# GIAC Certified Forensic Analyst Complete Self-Assessment Guide

The guidance in this Self-Assessment is base
Analyst best practices and standards in business process architecture, design and quality management. The guidance is also based on the professional judgment of the individual collaborators listed in the Acknowledgments.

## Notice of rights

## Trademarks

# Table of Contents

# About The Art of Service

The Art of Service, Business Process Architects since 2000, is dedicated to helping stakeholders achieve excellence.

Defining, designing, creating, and implementing a process to solve a stakeholders challenge or meet an objective is the most valuable role... In EVERY group, company, organization and department.

Unless you're talking a one-time, single-use project, there should be a process. Whether that process is managed and implemented by humans, AI, or a combination of the two, it needs to be designed by someone with a complex enough perspective to ask the right questions.

Someone capable of asking the right questions and step back and say, 'What are we really trying to accomplish here? And is there a different way to look at it?'

With The Art of Service's Standard Requirements Self-Assessments, we empower people who can do just that — whether their title is marketer, entrepreneur, manager, salesperson, consultant, Business Process Manager, executive assistant, IT Manager, CIO etc... —they are the people who rule the future. They are people who watch the process as it happens, and ask the right questions to make the process work better.

**Contact us when you need any support with this Self-Assessment and any help with templates, blue-prints and examples of standard documents you might need:**

http://theartofservice.com
service@theartofservice.com

# Acknowledgments

This checklist was developed under the auspices of The Art of Service, chaired by Gerardus Blokdyk.

Representatives from several client companies participated in the preparation of this Self-Assessment.

In addition, we are thankful for the design and printing services provided.

# Included Resources - how to access

Included with your purchase of the book is the GIAC Certified Forensic Analyst Self-Assessment Spreadsheet Dashboard which contains all questions and Self-Assessment areas and auto-generates insights, graphs, and project RACI planning - all with examples to get you started right away.

How? Simply send an email to
**access@theartofservice.com**
with this books' title in the subject to get the GIAC Certified Forensic Analyst Self Assessment Tool right away.

You will receive the following contents with New and Updated specific criteria:

• The latest quick edition of the book in PDF

• The latest complete edition of the book in PDF, which criteria correspond to the criteria in...

• The Self-Assessment Excel Dashboard, and...

• Example pre-filled Self-Assessment Excel Dashboard to get familiar with results generation

• In-depth specific Checklists covering the topic

• Project management checklists and templates to assist with implementation

**INCLUDES LIFETIME SELF ASSESSMENT UPDATES**

Every self assessment comes with Lifetime Updates and Lifetime Free Updated Books. Lifetime Updates is an industry-first feature which allows you to receive verified self assessment updates, ensuring you always have the most accurate information at your fingertips.

Get it now- you will be glad you did - do it now, before you forget.

Send an email to **access@theartofservice.com** with this books' title in the subject to get the GIAC Certified Forensic Analyst Self Assessment Tool right away.

# Your feedback is invaluable to us

If you recently bought this book, we would love to hear from you! You can do this by writing a review on amazon (or the online store where you purchased this book) about your last purchase! As part of our continual service improvement process, we love to hear real client experiences and feedback.

**How does it work?**
To post a review on Amazon, just log in to your account and click on the Create Your Own Review button (under Customer Reviews) of the relevant product page. You can find examples of product reviews in Amazon. If you purchased from another online store, simply follow their procedures.

**What happens when I submit my review?**
Once you have submitted your review, send us an email at review@theartofservice.com with the link to your review so we can properly thank you for your feedback.

# Purpose of this Self-Assessment

This Self-Assessment has been developed to improve understanding of the requirements and elements of GIAC Certified Forensic Analyst, based on best practices and standards in business process architecture, design and quality management.

It is designed to allow for a rapid Self-Assessment to determine how closely existing management practices and procedures correspond to the elements of the Self-Assessment.

The criteria of requirements and elements of GIAC Certified Forensic Analyst have been rephrased in the format of a Self-Assessment questionnaire, with a seven-criterion scoring system, as explained in this document.

In this format, even with limited background knowledge of GIAC

Certified Forensic Analyst, a manager can quickly review existing operations to determine how they measure up to the standards. This in turn can serve as the starting point of a 'gap analysis' to identify management tools or system elements that might usefully be implemented in the organization to help improve overall performance.

# How to use the Self-Assessment

On the following pages are a series of questions to identify to what extent your GIAC Certified Forensic Analyst initiative is complete in comparison to the requirements set in standards.

To facilitate answering the questions, there is a space in front of each question to enter a score on a scale of '1' to '5'.

1 Strongly Disagree

2 Disagree

3 Neutral

4 Agree

5 Strongly Agree

*Read the question and rate it with the following in front of mind:*

**'In my belief,
the answer to this question is clearly defined'.**

There are two ways in which you can choose to interpret this statement;
1. how aware are you that the answer to the question is clearly defined
2. for more in-depth analysis you can choose to gather

evidence and confirm the answer to the question. This obviously will take more time, most Self-Assessment users opt for the first way to interpret the question and dig deeper later on based on the outcome of the overall Self-Assessment.

A score of '1' would mean that the answer is not clear at all, where a '5' would mean the answer is crystal clear and defined. Leave emtpy when the question is not applicable or you don't want to answer it, you can skip it without affecting your score. Write your score in the space provided.

After you have responded to all the appropriate statements in each section, compute your average score for that section, using the formula provided, and round to the nearest tenth. Then transfer to the corresponding spoke in the GIAC Certified Forensic Analyst Scorecard on the second next page of the Self-Assessment.

Your completed GIAC Certified Forensic Analyst Scorecard will give you a clear presentation of which GIAC Certified Forensic Analyst areas need attention.

# GIAC Certified Forensic Analyst Scorecard Example

Example of how the finalized Scorecard can look like:

# GIAC Certified Forensic Analyst Scorecard

Your Scores:

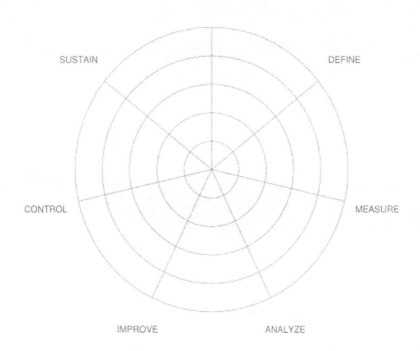

# BEGINNING OF THE SELF-ASSESSMENT:

# CRITERION #1: RECOGNIZE

INTENT: Be aware of the need for change. Recognize that there is an unfavorable variation, problem or symptom.

In my belief, the answer to this question is clearly defined:

5 Strongly Agree

4 Agree

3 Neutral

2 Disagree

1 Strongly Disagree

1. What are the minority interests and what amount of minority interests can be recognized?
<--- Score

2. What are the expected benefits of GIAC Certified Forensic Analyst to the business?
<--- Score

3. Are controls defined to recognize and contain

problems?
<--- Score

4. Are there GIAC Certified Forensic Analyst problems defined?
<--- Score

5. For your GIAC Certified Forensic Analyst project, identify and describe the business environment, is there more than one layer to the business environment?
<--- Score

6. What vendors make products that address the GIAC Certified Forensic Analyst needs?
<--- Score

7. What needs to be done?
<--- Score

8. To what extent would your organization benefit from being recognized as a award recipient?
<--- Score

9. What are the timeframes required to resolve each of the issues/problems?
<--- Score

10. What is the problem or issue?
<--- Score

11. Are you dealing with any of the same issues today as yesterday? What can you do about this?
<--- Score

12. How does it fit into your organizational needs and

tasks?
<--- Score

13. How are the GIAC Certified Forensic Analyst's objectives aligned to the organization's overall business strategy?
<--- Score

14. Can management personnel recognize the monetary benefit of GIAC Certified Forensic Analyst?
<--- Score

15. Are your goals realistic? Do you need to redefine your problem? Perhaps the problem has changed or maybe you have reached your goal and need to set a new one?
<--- Score

16. Looking at each person individually – does every one have the qualities which are needed to work in this group?
<--- Score

17. Are there any revenue recognition issues?
<--- Score

18. What are the business objectives to be achieved with GIAC Certified Forensic Analyst?
<--- Score

19. Are there recognized GIAC Certified Forensic Analyst problems?
<--- Score

20. Will it solve real problems?
<--- Score

21. To what extent does each concerned units management team recognize GIAC Certified Forensic Analyst as an effective investment?

<--- Score

22. How do you take a forward-looking perspective in identifying GIAC Certified Forensic Analyst research related to market response and models?

<--- Score

23. What training and capacity building actions are needed to implement proposed reforms?

<--- Score

24. How much are sponsors, customers, partners, stakeholders involved in GIAC Certified Forensic Analyst? In other words, what are the risks, if GIAC Certified Forensic Analyst does not deliver successfully?

<--- Score

25. Do you need to avoid or amend any GIAC Certified Forensic Analyst activities?

<--- Score

26. What extra resources will you need?

<--- Score

27. Will a response program recognize when a crisis occurs and provide some level of response?

<--- Score

28. How do you identify the kinds of information that you will need?

<--- Score

29. Is the need for organizational change recognized?
<--- Score

30. Who else hopes to benefit from it?
<--- Score

31. What else needs to be measured?
<--- Score

32. How can auditing be a preventative security measure?
<--- Score

33. What situation(s) led to this GIAC Certified Forensic Analyst Self Assessment?
<--- Score

34. How are you going to measure success?
<--- Score

35. Does your organization need more GIAC Certified Forensic Analyst education?
<--- Score

36. How do you assess your GIAC Certified Forensic Analyst workforce capability and capacity needs, including skills, competencies, and staffing levels?
<--- Score

37. Are employees recognized or rewarded for performance that demonstrates the highest levels of integrity?
<--- Score

38. What information do users need?

<--- Score

39. Who needs to know about GIAC Certified Forensic Analyst?
<--- Score

40. Will GIAC Certified Forensic Analyst deliverables need to be tested and, if so, by whom?
<--- Score

41. What should be considered when identifying available resources, constraints, and deadlines?
<--- Score

42. When a GIAC Certified Forensic Analyst manager recognizes a problem, what options are available?
<--- Score

43. What are your needs in relation to GIAC Certified Forensic Analyst skills, labor, equipment, and markets?
<--- Score

44. As a sponsor, customer or management, how important is it to meet goals, objectives?
<--- Score

45. Is it clear when you think of the day ahead of you what activities and tasks you need to complete?
<--- Score

46. Do you know what you need to know about GIAC Certified Forensic Analyst?
<--- Score

47. Are problem definition and motivation clearly presented?

<--- Score

48. What problems are you facing and how do you consider GIAC Certified Forensic Analyst will circumvent those obstacles?
<--- Score

49. What prevents you from making the changes you know will make you a more effective GIAC Certified Forensic Analyst leader?
<--- Score

50. Are there any specific expectations or concerns about the GIAC Certified Forensic Analyst team, GIAC Certified Forensic Analyst itself?
<--- Score

51. What is the smallest subset of the problem you can usefully solve?
<--- Score

52. Will new equipment/products be required to facilitate GIAC Certified Forensic Analyst delivery, for example is new software needed?
<--- Score

53. What tools and technologies are needed for a custom GIAC Certified Forensic Analyst project?
<--- Score

54. Does GIAC Certified Forensic Analyst create potential expectations in other areas that need to be recognized and considered?
<--- Score

55. Who are your key stakeholders who need to sign

off?

<--- Score

**56. What preventative corrective actions should you implement?**

<--- Score

57. Who had the original idea?

<--- Score

58. Who needs what information?

<--- Score

59. What does GIAC Certified Forensic Analyst success mean to the stakeholders?

<--- Score

60. Think about the people you identified for your GIAC Certified Forensic Analyst project and the project responsibilities you would assign to them. what kind of training do you think they would need to perform these responsibilities effectively?

<--- Score

61. Do you have/need 24-hour access to key personnel?

<--- Score

**62. How do entities determine which events constitute a breach requiring customer notification?**

<--- Score

63. Consider your own GIAC Certified Forensic Analyst project, what types of organizational problems do you think might be causing or affecting your problem,

based on the work done so far?
<--- Score

64. Should you invest in industry-recognized qualications?
<--- Score

65. Who defines the rules in relation to any given issue?
<--- Score

66. What would happen if GIAC Certified Forensic Analyst weren't done?
<--- Score

67. Do you need different information or graphics?
<--- Score

68. What do you need to start doing?
<--- Score

Add up total points for this section:
_ _ _ _ _  = Total points for this section

Divided by: _ _ _ _ _ _ (number of statements answered) = _ _ _ _ _ _
Average score for this section

Transfer your score to the GIAC Certified Forensic Analyst Index at the beginning of the Self-Assessment.

# CRITERION #2: DEFINE:

INTENT: Formulate the business problem. Define the problem, needs and objectives.

In my belief, the answer to this question is clearly defined:

5 Strongly Agree

4 Agree

3 Neutral

2 Disagree

1 Strongly Disagree

1. Is the GIAC Certified Forensic Analyst scope manageable?
<--- Score

2. Is the team adequately staffed with the desired cross-functionality? If not, what additional resources are available to the team?
<--- Score

3. What system do you use for gathering GIAC Certified Forensic Analyst information?
<--- Score

4. What are the tasks and definitions?
<--- Score

5. Has a high-level 'as is' process map been completed, verified and validated?
<--- Score

6. Are different versions of process maps needed to account for the different types of inputs?
<--- Score

7. Why are you doing GIAC Certified Forensic Analyst and what is the scope?
<--- Score

8. How do you gather GIAC Certified Forensic Analyst requirements?
<--- Score

9. Has everyone on the team, including the team leaders, been properly trained?
<--- Score

10. How often are the team meetings?
<--- Score

11. Who are the GIAC Certified Forensic Analyst improvement team members, including Management Leads and Coaches?
<--- Score

12. In what way can you redefine the criteria of choice

clients have in your category in your favor?
<--- Score

13. Scope of sensitive information?
<--- Score

14. Have all of the relationships been defined properly?
<--- Score

15. Has a project plan, Gantt chart, or similar been developed/completed?
<--- Score

16. What happens if GIAC Certified Forensic Analyst's scope changes?
<--- Score

17. What baselines are required to be defined and managed?
<--- Score

18. What specifically is the problem? Where does it occur? When does it occur? What is its extent?
<--- Score

19. What was the context?
<--- Score

20. What defines best in class?
<--- Score

21. What is out of scope?
<--- Score

22. Is the GIAC Certified Forensic Analyst scope

complete and appropriately sized?
<--- Score

23. How and when will the baselines be defined?
<--- Score

24. Has the improvement team collected the 'voice of the customer' (obtained feedback – qualitative and quantitative)?
<--- Score

25. Are customer(s) identified and segmented according to their different needs and requirements?
<--- Score

26. How will variation in the actual durations of each activity be dealt with to ensure that the expected GIAC Certified Forensic Analyst results are met?
<--- Score

27. Is GIAC Certified Forensic Analyst currently on schedule according to the plan?
<--- Score

28. Have specific policy objectives been defined?
<--- Score

29. Are customers identified and high impact areas defined?
<--- Score

30. How will the GIAC Certified Forensic Analyst team and the organization measure complete success of GIAC Certified Forensic Analyst?
<--- Score

31. Are roles and responsibilities formally defined?
<--- Score

32. What GIAC Certified Forensic Analyst requirements should be gathered?
<--- Score

33. Is it clearly defined in and to your organization what you do?
<--- Score

34. Have the customer needs been translated into specific, measurable requirements? How?
<--- Score

35. What would be the goal or target for a GIAC Certified Forensic Analyst's improvement team?
<--- Score

36. Is GIAC Certified Forensic Analyst required?
<--- Score

37. Is the current 'as is' process being followed? If not, what are the discrepancies?
<--- Score

38. Are resources adequate for the scope?
<--- Score

39. Does the team have regular meetings?
<--- Score

40. How did the GIAC Certified Forensic Analyst manager receive input to the development of a GIAC Certified Forensic Analyst improvement plan and the estimated completion dates/times of each activity?

<--- Score

41. What is the definition of success?
<--- Score

42. Is full participation by members in regularly held team meetings guaranteed?
<--- Score

43. Do the problem and goal statements meet the SMART criteria (specific, measurable, attainable, relevant, and time-bound)?
<--- Score

44. What critical content must be communicated – who, what, when, where, and how?
<--- Score

45. What are the boundaries of the scope? What is in bounds and what is not? What is the start point? What is the stop point?
<--- Score

46. What key business process output measure(s) does GIAC Certified Forensic Analyst leverage and how?
<--- Score

47. How does the GIAC Certified Forensic Analyst manager ensure against scope creep?
<--- Score

48. How do you hand over GIAC Certified Forensic Analyst context?
<--- Score

49. Are business processes mapped?

<--- Score

50. Has/have the customer(s) been identified?
<--- Score

51. How do you manage scope?
<--- Score

52. Has the GIAC Certified Forensic Analyst work been fairly and/or equitably divided and delegated among team members who are qualified and capable to perform the work? Has everyone contributed?
<--- Score

53. Are approval levels defined for contracts and supplements to contracts?
<--- Score

54. If substitutes have been appointed, have they been briefed on the GIAC Certified Forensic Analyst goals and received regular communications as to the progress to date?
<--- Score

55. Is data collected and displayed to better understand customer(s) critical needs and requirements.
<--- Score

56. How do you keep key subject matter experts in the loop?
<--- Score

57. Are team charters developed?
<--- Score

58. What is the context?
<--- Score

59. Does the scope remain the same?
<--- Score

60. Is GIAC Certified Forensic Analyst linked to key business goals and objectives?
<--- Score

61. Has the direction changed at all during the course of GIAC Certified Forensic Analyst? If so, when did it change and why?
<--- Score

62. Is the improvement team aware of the different versions of a process: what they think it is vs. what it actually is vs. what it should be vs. what it could be?
<--- Score

63. Is there a GIAC Certified Forensic Analyst management charter, including business case, problem and goal statements, scope, milestones, roles and responsibilities, communication plan?
<--- Score

64. Will team members regularly document their GIAC Certified Forensic Analyst work?
<--- Score

65. Has a team charter been developed and communicated?
<--- Score

66. Is a fully trained team formed, supported, and committed to work on the GIAC Certified Forensic

Analyst improvements?

<--- Score

67. What is the scope of GIAC Certified Forensic Analyst?

<--- Score

68. Is there regularly 100% attendance at the team meetings? If not, have appointed substitutes attended to preserve cross-functionality and full representation?

<--- Score

69. How is the team tracking and documenting its work?

<--- Score

70. What are the rough order estimates on cost savings/opportunities that GIAC Certified Forensic Analyst brings?

<--- Score

71. When are meeting minutes sent out? Who is on the distribution list?

<--- Score

72. Are required metrics defined, what are they?

<--- Score

73. What are the dynamics of the communication plan?

<--- Score

74. What are the record-keeping requirements of GIAC Certified Forensic Analyst activities?

<--- Score

75. Is there a completed SIPOC representation, describing the Suppliers, Inputs, Process, Outputs, and Customers?
<--- Score

76. How can the value of GIAC Certified Forensic Analyst be defined?
<--- Score

77. When is the estimated completion date?
<--- Score

78. Are accountability and ownership for GIAC Certified Forensic Analyst clearly defined?
<--- Score

79. Are there different segments of customers?
<--- Score

80. How was the 'as is' process map developed, reviewed, verified and validated?
<--- Score

81. What is out-of-scope initially?
<--- Score

82. How would you define the culture at your organization, how susceptible is it to GIAC Certified Forensic Analyst changes?
<--- Score

83. Is the team sponsored by a champion or business leader?
<--- Score

84. What customer feedback methods were used to solicit their input?
<--- Score

85. Are improvement team members fully trained on GIAC Certified Forensic Analyst?
<--- Score

86. Is there a completed, verified, and validated high-level 'as is' (not 'should be' or 'could be') business process map?
<--- Score

87. When was the GIAC Certified Forensic Analyst start date?
<--- Score

88. Will team members perform GIAC Certified Forensic Analyst work when assigned and in a timely fashion?
<--- Score

89. Have all basic functions of GIAC Certified Forensic Analyst been defined?
<--- Score

90. Do you all define GIAC Certified Forensic Analyst in the same way?
<--- Score

91. Who is gathering GIAC Certified Forensic Analyst information?
<--- Score

92. What are the Roles and Responsibilities for each team member and its leadership? Where is this

documented?
<--- Score

93. Is the team equipped with available and reliable resources?
<--- Score

94. What is the scope of the GIAC Certified Forensic Analyst effort?
<--- Score

95. Has your scope been defined?
<--- Score

96. Is there a critical path to deliver GIAC Certified Forensic Analyst results?
<--- Score

97. Who defines (or who defined) the rules and roles?
<--- Score

98. What are the compelling business reasons for embarking on GIAC Certified Forensic Analyst?
<--- Score

99. What constraints exist that might impact the team?
<--- Score

100. Is the team formed and are team leaders (Coaches and Management Leads) assigned?
<--- Score

101. What scope to assess?
<--- Score

102. What is in the scope and what is not in scope?
<--- Score

103. Is scope creep really all bad news?
<--- Score

104. Are task requirements clearly defined?
<--- Score

105. What sources do you use to gather information for a GIAC Certified Forensic Analyst study?
<--- Score

106. Are there any constraints known that bear on the ability to perform GIAC Certified Forensic Analyst work? How is the team addressing them?
<--- Score

107. Has anyone else (internal or external to the organization) attempted to solve this problem or a similar one before? If so, what knowledge can be leveraged from these previous efforts?
<--- Score

108. Is the scope of GIAC Certified Forensic Analyst defined?
<--- Score

109. Are audit criteria, scope, frequency and methods defined?
<--- Score

110. What is in scope?
<--- Score

111. How do you think the partners involved in

GIAC Certified Forensic Analyst would have defined success?
<--- Score

Add up total points for this section:
_____ = Total points for this section

Divided by: _____ (number of statements answered) = _____
Average score for this section

Transfer your score to the GIAC Certified Forensic Analyst Index at the beginning of the Self-Assessment.

# CRITERION #3: MEASURE:

INTENT: Gather the correct data.
Measure the current performance and
evolution of the situation.

In my belief, the answer to this
question is clearly defined:

5 Strongly Agree

4 Agree

3 Neutral

2 Disagree

1 Strongly Disagree

1. How are measurements made?
<--- Score

2. How do you measure success?
<--- Score

3. Does the GIAC Certified Forensic Analyst task fit the client's priorities?
<--- Score

4. Who participated in the data collection for measurements?
<--- Score

5. What relevant entities could be measured?
<--- Score

6. What could cause you to change course?
<--- Score

7. What data was collected (past, present, future/ ongoing)?
<--- Score

8. Do you effectively measure and reward individual and team performance?
<--- Score

9. How will you measure your GIAC Certified Forensic Analyst effectiveness?
<--- Score

10. Can you do GIAC Certified Forensic Analyst without complex (expensive) analysis?
<--- Score

11. Are high impact defects defined and identified in the business process?
<--- Score

12. What are the uncertainties surrounding estimates of impact?
<--- Score

13. Are key measures identified and agreed upon?

<--- Score

14. Is key measure data collection planned
and executed, process variation displayed and
communicated and performance baselined?
<--- Score

15. How do you measure efficient delivery of GIAC
Certified Forensic Analyst services?
<--- Score

16. Why do you expend time and effort to implement
measurement, for whom?
<--- Score

17. How do you focus on what is right -not who is
right?
<--- Score

18. What causes innovation to fail or succeed in your
organization?
<--- Score

19. Are losses documented, analyzed, and remedial
processes developed to prevent future losses?
<--- Score

20. Is the solution cost-effective?
<--- Score

21. What evidence is there and what is measured?
<--- Score

22. How can you measure GIAC Certified Forensic
Analyst in a systematic way?
<--- Score

23. Do you aggressively reward and promote the people who have the biggest impact on creating excellent GIAC Certified Forensic Analyst services/products?
<--- Score

24. How can you measure the performance?
<--- Score

25. Why do the measurements/indicators matter?
<--- Score

26. What could cause delays in the schedule?
<--- Score

27. Where is it measured?
<--- Score

28. Which stakeholder characteristics are analyzed?
<--- Score

29. How do you measure variability?
<--- Score

30. Are you taking your company in the direction of better and revenue or cheaper and cost?
<--- Score

31. What methods are feasible and acceptable to estimate the impact of reforms?
<--- Score

32. What do you measure and why?
<--- Score

33. Who should receive measurement reports?
<--- Score

34. What particular quality tools did the team find helpful in establishing measurements?
<--- Score

35. What are your key GIAC Certified Forensic Analyst organizational performance measures, including key short and longer-term financial measures?
<--- Score

36. Does GIAC Certified Forensic Analyst analysis isolate the fundamental causes of problems?
<--- Score

37. How do you aggregate measures across priorities?
<--- Score

38. What key measures identified indicate the performance of the business process?
<--- Score

39. What are your key GIAC Certified Forensic Analyst indicators that you will measure, analyze and track?
<--- Score

40. Does GIAC Certified Forensic Analyst systematically track and analyze outcomes for accountability and quality improvement?
<--- Score

41. How will measures be used to manage and adapt?
<--- Score

42. Is a solid data collection plan established that

includes measurement systems analysis?

<--- Score

43. Have changes been properly/adequately analyzed for effect?

<--- Score

44. How do you control the overall costs of your work processes?

<--- Score

45. Does GIAC Certified Forensic Analyst analysis show the relationships among important GIAC Certified Forensic Analyst factors?

<--- Score

46. Among the GIAC Certified Forensic Analyst product and service cost to be estimated, which is considered hardest to estimate?

<--- Score

47. How large is the gap between current performance and the customer-specified (goal) performance?

<--- Score

48. What causes investor action?

<--- Score

49. Is data collection planned and executed?

<--- Score

50. What harm might be caused?

<--- Score

51. Does your organization systematically track and

analyze outcomes related for accountability and quality improvement?
<--- Score

52. What are your customers expectations and measures?
<--- Score

53. What is the right balance of time and resources between investigation, analysis, and discussion and dissemination?
<--- Score

54. How frequently do you track GIAC Certified Forensic Analyst measures?
<--- Score

55. What has the team done to assure the stability and accuracy of the measurement process?
<--- Score

56. Is long term and short term variability accounted for?
<--- Score

57. How is progress measured?
<--- Score

58. What are the costs of reform?
<--- Score

59. Did you tackle the cause or the symptom?
<--- Score

60. Do staff have the necessary skills to collect, analyze, and report data?

<--- Score

**61. What are the costs to companies of the data breaches that occurred?**
<--- Score

62. What is measured? Why?
<--- Score

63. Is data collected on key measures that were identified?
<--- Score

64. How is performance measured?
<--- Score

65. Have you found any 'ground fruit' or 'low-hanging fruit' for immediate remedies to the gap in performance?
<--- Score

66. What are the agreed upon definitions of the high impact areas, defect(s), unit(s), and opportunities that will figure into the process capability metrics?
<--- Score

67. What are the key input variables? What are the key process variables? What are the key output variables?
<--- Score

68. How will your organization measure success?
<--- Score

69. Have you made assumptions about the shape of the future, particularly its impact on your customers and competitors?

<--- Score

70. Are missed GIAC Certified Forensic Analyst opportunities costing your organization money?
<--- Score

71. Is Process Variation Displayed/Communicated?
<--- Score

72. How do you do risk analysis of rare, cascading, catastrophic events?
<--- Score

73. Are there measurements based on task performance?
<--- Score

74. Are you aware of what could cause a problem?
<--- Score

75. Are process variation components displayed/ communicated using suitable charts, graphs, plots?
<--- Score

76. What potential environmental factors impact the GIAC Certified Forensic Analyst effort?
<--- Score

77. How is the value delivered by GIAC Certified Forensic Analyst being measured?
<--- Score

78. What are the types and number of measures to use?
<--- Score

79. Which measures and indicators matter?
<--- Score

80. Are the units of measure consistent?
<--- Score

81. How to cause the change?
<--- Score

82. Have the concerns of stakeholders to help identify and define potential barriers been obtained and analyzed?
<--- Score

83. What is an unallowable cost?
<--- Score

**84. Where should mitigation efforts be focused?**
<--- Score

85. How do your measurements capture actionable GIAC Certified Forensic Analyst information for use in exceeding your customers expectations and securing your customers engagement?
<--- Score

86. How will effects be measured?
<--- Score

87. The approach of traditional GIAC Certified Forensic Analyst works for detail complexity but is focused on a systematic approach rather than an understanding of the nature of systems themselves, what approach will permit your organization to deal with the kind of unpredictable emergent behaviors that dynamic complexity can introduce?

<--- Score

88. Are the measurements objective?
<--- Score

89. What measurements are being captured?
<--- Score

90. Can you measure the return on analysis?
<--- Score

91. How do you know that any GIAC Certified Forensic Analyst analysis is complete and comprehensive?
<--- Score

92. What charts has the team used to display the components of variation in the process?
<--- Score

93. What causes extra work or rework?
<--- Score

94. How will success or failure be measured?
<--- Score

95. What causes mismanagement?
<--- Score

96. How do you stay flexible and focused to recognize larger GIAC Certified Forensic Analyst results?
<--- Score

97. How do you measure lifecycle phases?
<--- Score

98. Is it possible to estimate the impact of

unanticipated complexity such as wrong or failed assumptions, feedback, etc. on proposed reforms?
<--- Score

99. How do you identify and analyze stakeholders and their interests?
<--- Score

100. Are there any easy-to-implement alternatives to GIAC Certified Forensic Analyst? Sometimes other solutions are available that do not require the cost implications of a full-blown project?
<--- Score

101. Is there a Performance Baseline?
<--- Score

102. Was a data collection plan established?
<--- Score

103. What measurements are possible, practicable and meaningful?
<--- Score

104. What would be a real cause for concern?
<--- Score

105. Have all non-recommended alternatives been analyzed in sufficient detail?
<--- Score

106. Have the types of risks that may impact GIAC Certified Forensic Analyst been identified and analyzed?
<--- Score

107. How will you measure success?
<--- Score

108. What disadvantage does this cause for the user?
<--- Score

Add up total points for this section:
_ _ _ _ _ = Total points for this section

Divided by: _ _ _ _ _ _ (number of
statements answered) = _ _ _ _ _ _
Average score for this section

Transfer your score to the GIAC Certified
Forensic Analyst Index at the beginning
of the Self-Assessment.

# CRITERION #4: ANALYZE:

INTENT: Analyze causes, assumptions and hypotheses.

In my belief, the answer to this question is clearly defined:

5 Strongly Agree

4 Agree

3 Neutral

2 Disagree

1 Strongly Disagree

1. What successful thing are you doing today that may be blinding you to new growth opportunities?
<--- Score

2. Do your contracts/agreements contain data security obligations?
<--- Score

**3. Could the data be provided to unauthorized users without the knowledge of your**

**organization?**

<--- Score

4. How often will data be collected for measures?

<--- Score

5. Is the suppliers process defined and controlled?

<--- Score

6. Is the GIAC Certified Forensic Analyst process severely broken such that a re-design is necessary?

<--- Score

**7. Which data breach lawsuits settle?**

<--- Score

**8. Who is behind data breaches?**

<--- Score

9. What are your key performance measures or indicators and in-process measures for the control and improvement of your GIAC Certified Forensic Analyst processes?

<--- Score

10. What quality tools were used to get through the analyze phase?

<--- Score

**11. Do states have laws that requiring data breach notifications to the affected parties?**

<--- Score

12. What tools were used to generate the list of possible causes?

<--- Score

13. What were the crucial 'moments of truth' on the process map?

<--- Score

**14. Is IT System or Data Sensitive?**

<--- Score

**15. How is the data stored in your organization?**

<--- Score

**16. What are the consequences if your data is breached?**

<--- Score

17. What conclusions were drawn from the team's data collection and analysis? How did the team reach these conclusions?

<--- Score

**18. Are you sure you can detect data breaches?**

<--- Score

**19. How many people have access to the data?**

<--- Score

20. What other jobs or tasks affect the performance of the steps in the GIAC Certified Forensic Analyst process?

<--- Score

21. What are the best opportunities for value improvement?

<--- Score

22. Record-keeping requirements flow from the

records needed as inputs, outputs, controls and for transformation of a GIAC Certified Forensic Analyst process. Are the records needed as inputs to the GIAC Certified Forensic Analyst process available?

<--- Score

23. What methods do you use to gather GIAC Certified Forensic Analyst data?

<--- Score

24. What are your current levels and trends in key measures or indicators of GIAC Certified Forensic Analyst product and process performance that are important to and directly serve your customers? How do these results compare with the performance of your competitors and other organizations with similar offerings?

<--- Score

25. What other organizational variables, such as reward systems or communication systems, affect the performance of this GIAC Certified Forensic Analyst process?

<--- Score

**26. If data is transported, how it is transported?**

<--- Score

27. Where is the data coming from to measure compliance?

<--- Score

**28. What type of controls does your organization have over the data given to developers?**

<--- Score

29. What is the cost of poor quality as supported by the team's analysis?
<--- Score

30. What controls do you have in place to protect data?
<--- Score

31. Did any value-added analysis or 'lean thinking' take place to identify some of the gaps shown on the 'as is' process map?
<--- Score

32. How do you identify specific GIAC Certified Forensic Analyst investment opportunities and emerging trends?
<--- Score

**33. What Happens When Data Gets Hacked?**
<--- Score

34. How do mission and objectives affect the GIAC Certified Forensic Analyst processes of your organization?
<--- Score

35. Is the performance gap determined?
<--- Score

**36. How Could the Data Be Used?**
<--- Score

**37. Can you guarantee the security of the data and that it will not be lost, stolen, or shared with unauthorized parties or individuals?**
<--- Score

**38. Does your organization receive or possess data with personal information/identifiers?**
<--- Score

39. What data is gathered?
<--- Score

40. Was a detailed process map created to amplify critical steps of the 'as is' business process?
<--- Score

**41. Which data breaches are being litigated?**
<--- Score

42. How do you promote understanding that opportunity for improvement is not criticism of the status quo, or the people who created the status quo?
<--- Score

43. What were the financial benefits resulting from any 'ground fruit or low-hanging fruit' (quick fixes)?
<--- Score

**44. What data is private?**
<--- Score

45. Do your employees have the opportunity to do what they do best everyday?
<--- Score

46. Identify an operational issue in your organization. for example, could a particular task be done more quickly or more efficiently by GIAC Certified Forensic Analyst?
<--- Score

47. What GIAC Certified Forensic Analyst data do you gather or use now?

<--- Score

**48. What kind of data can be lost?**

<--- Score

49. How do your work systems and key work processes relate to and capitalize on your core competencies?

<--- Score

50. What does the data say about the performance of the business process?

<--- Score

51. Think about some of the processes you undertake within your organization, which do you own?

<--- Score

**52. During a timeframe when a data breach occurred, what other third party research applications were also able to access the data of unsuspecting users?**

<--- Score

53. An organizationally feasible system request is one that considers the mission, goals and objectives of the organization. Key questions are: is the GIAC Certified Forensic Analyst solution request practical and will it solve a problem or take advantage of an opportunity to achieve company goals?

<--- Score

54. Have the problem and goal statements been

updated to reflect the additional knowledge gained from the analyze phase?
<--- Score

### 55. Data breach notification: what to do when your personal data has been breached?
<--- Score

### 56. Which Data Breaches are Litigated in Federal Court?
<--- Score

57. What are your GIAC Certified Forensic Analyst processes?
<--- Score

### 58. What type of controls do you have over the data given to developers?
<--- Score

### 59. Does the data ever leave your facility on a laptop or in some other form?
<--- Score

60. What did the team gain from developing a sub-process map?
<--- Score

### 61. What constitutes a data breach?
<--- Score

### 62. Which data breaches are litigated?
<--- Score

63. Can you add value to the current GIAC Certified Forensic Analyst decision-making process (largely

qualitative) by incorporating uncertainty modeling (more quantitative)?

<--- Score

**64. Do you have protective safeguards in place, including audits, to ensure developers were not misusing the users data?**

<--- Score

65. What are the revised rough estimates of the financial savings/opportunity for GIAC Certified Forensic Analyst improvements?

<--- Score

66. Is the gap/opportunity displayed and communicated in financial terms?

<--- Score

**67. If a data breach occurs in an online system, how do you know if its a real breach or a rumor of a breach?**

<--- Score

68. Are GIAC Certified Forensic Analyst changes recognized early enough to be approved through the regular process?

<--- Score

69. How do you implement and manage your work processes to ensure that they meet design requirements?

<--- Score

70. Do you, as a leader, bounce back quickly from setbacks?

<--- Score

71. Were any designed experiments used to generate additional insight into the data analysis?
<--- Score

72. What process should you select for improvement?
<--- Score

73. Is Data and process analysis, root cause analysis and quantifying the gap/opportunity in place?
<--- Score

74. Do several people in different organizational units assist with the GIAC Certified Forensic Analyst process?
<--- Score

**75. If a breach occurs or the regulator investigates the organization; you need to have documents to explain the complete data flows. Are you ready to answer those questions as the level of fines will take into account the processes; technology; and documentation that describes the systems and flow of data. Are you ready for that?**
<--- Score

**76. What data does your device/system capture?**
<--- Score

77. What is your organizations process which leads to recognition of value generation?
<--- Score

**78. Can You Leave It To Your IT Department To Sanitize Data?**
<--- Score

### 79. So What Do You Do To Safeguard Data?
<--- Score

80. Is the required GIAC Certified Forensic Analyst data gathered?
<--- Score

81. Were there any improvement opportunities identified from the process analysis?
<--- Score

82. What are your current levels and trends in key GIAC Certified Forensic Analyst measures or indicators of product and process performance that are important to and directly serve your customers?
<--- Score

83. Think about the functions involved in your GIAC Certified Forensic Analyst project, what processes flow from these functions?
<--- Score

84. Were Pareto charts (or similar) used to portray the 'heavy hitters' (or key sources of variation)?
<--- Score

85. How does the organization define, manage, and improve its GIAC Certified Forensic Analyst processes?
<--- Score

### 86. How Do Data Breaches Occur ?
<--- Score

87. Was a cause-and-effect diagram used to explore the different types of causes (or sources of variation)?

<--- Score

88. Have any additional benefits been identified that will result from closing all or most of the gaps?
<--- Score

89. Where is GIAC Certified Forensic Analyst data gathered?
<--- Score

**90. Are your organizations user terms of service and data clear and understandable?**
<--- Score

**91. Can companies immunize themselves from cyber-attacks and data breaches?**
<--- Score

**92. What type of data can be stolen (account #, expiry date, track data, CVV2,PIN, SS#, etc.)?**
<--- Score

93. A compounding model resolution with available relevant data can often provide insight towards a solution methodology; which GIAC Certified Forensic Analyst models, tools and techniques are necessary?
<--- Score

94. Are gaps between current performance and the goal performance identified?
<--- Score

**95. Who is responsible for a data breach?**
<--- Score

96. How do you measure the operational performance

of your key work systems and processes, including productivity, cycle time, and other appropriate measures of process effectiveness, efficiency, and innovation?
<--- Score

97. How is GIAC Certified Forensic Analyst data gathered?
<--- Score

98. How is the way you as the leader think and process information affecting your organizational culture?
<--- Score

99. How do you use GIAC Certified Forensic Analyst data and information to support organizational decision making and innovation?
<--- Score

100. What are your best practices for minimizing GIAC Certified Forensic Analyst project risk, while demonstrating incremental value and quick wins throughout the GIAC Certified Forensic Analyst project lifecycle?
<--- Score

101. Did any additional data need to be collected?
<--- Score

102. Do your leaders quickly bounce back from setbacks?
<--- Score

103. How was the detailed process map generated, verified, and validated?
<--- Score

**104. What kinds of data breaches are being litigated in federal court, and why?**
<--- Score

105. What tools were used to narrow the list of possible causes?
<--- Score

Add up total points for this section:
_ _ _ _ _ = Total points for this section

Divided by: _ _ _ _ _ _ (number of statements answered) = _ _ _ _ _ _
Average score for this section

Transfer your score to the GIAC Certified Forensic Analyst Index at the beginning of the Self-Assessment.

# CRITERION #5: IMPROVE:

INTENT: Develop a practical solution. Innovate, establish and test the solution and to measure the results.

In my belief, the answer to this question is clearly defined:

5 Strongly Agree

4 Agree

3 Neutral

2 Disagree

1 Strongly Disagree

1. What resources are required for the improvement efforts?
<--- Score

2. Is the solution technically practical?
<--- Score

3. In the past few months, what is the smallest change you have made that has had the biggest positive

result? What was it about that small change that produced the large return?
<--- Score

4. Who controls the risk?
<--- Score

5. What lessons, if any, from a pilot were incorporated into the design of the full-scale solution?
<--- Score

6. How can skill-level changes improve GIAC Certified Forensic Analyst?
<--- Score

7. For estimation problems, how do you develop an estimation statement?
<--- Score

8. How will you know that a change is an improvement?
<--- Score

9. Explorations of the frontiers of GIAC Certified Forensic Analyst will help you build influence, improve GIAC Certified Forensic Analyst, optimize decision making, and sustain change, what is your approach?
<--- Score

10. What error proofing will be done to address some of the discrepancies observed in the 'as is' process?
<--- Score

11. Risk factors: what are the characteristics of GIAC Certified Forensic Analyst that make it risky?

<--- Score

12. How do you measure risk?
<--- Score

13. Is the measure of success for GIAC Certified Forensic Analyst understandable to a variety of people?
<--- Score

14. Is the implementation plan designed?
<--- Score

15. Is there a small-scale pilot for proposed improvement(s)? What conclusions were drawn from the outcomes of a pilot?
<--- Score

16. What improvements have been achieved?
<--- Score

17. Are there any constraints (technical, political, cultural, or otherwise) that would inhibit certain solutions?
<--- Score

18. Is the optimal solution selected based on testing and analysis?
<--- Score

19. Was a pilot designed for the proposed solution(s)?
<--- Score

20. What is GIAC Certified Forensic Analyst's impact on utilizing the best solution(s)?
<--- Score

21. What actually has to improve and by how much?
<--- Score

22. What is the magnitude of the improvements?
<--- Score

23. How do you keep improving GIAC Certified
Forensic Analyst?
<--- Score

24. What are the implications of the one critical GIAC
Certified Forensic Analyst decision 10 minutes, 10
months, and 10 years from now?
<--- Score

25. Risk events: what are the things that could go
wrong?
<--- Score

26. Is a contingency plan established?
<--- Score

27. Does the goal represent a desired result that can
be measured?
<--- Score

28. What do you want to improve?
<--- Score

29. How do you measure progress and evaluate
training effectiveness?
<--- Score

30. If you could go back in time five years, what
decision would you make differently? What is your

best guess as to what decision you're making today you might regret five years from now?

<--- Score

31. How significant is the improvement in the eyes of the end user?

<--- Score

32. How do you improve your likelihood of success ?

<--- Score

33. How do you improve GIAC Certified Forensic Analyst service perception, and satisfaction?

<--- Score

34. Is pilot data collected and analyzed?

<--- Score

35. Who are the people involved in developing and implementing GIAC Certified Forensic Analyst?

<--- Score

36. Can the solution be designed and implemented within an acceptable time period?

<--- Score

37. What to do with the results or outcomes of measurements?

<--- Score

38. How do you link measurement and risk?

<--- Score

39. Will the controls trigger any other risks?

<--- Score

40. What tools were most useful during the improve phase?
<--- Score

41. What were the underlying assumptions on the cost-benefit analysis?
<--- Score

42. Were any criteria developed to assist the team in testing and evaluating potential solutions?
<--- Score

43. How will you know when its improved?
<--- Score

44. What is the implementation plan?
<--- Score

45. How do you improve productivity?
<--- Score

46. Who will be using the results of the measurement activities?
<--- Score

47. How will the team or the process owner(s) monitor the implementation plan to see that it is working as intended?
<--- Score

48. Why improve in the first place?
<--- Score

49. Who will be responsible for making the decisions to include or exclude requested changes once GIAC Certified Forensic Analyst is underway?

<--- Score

50. What needs improvement? Why?
<--- Score

51. How can you improve GIAC Certified Forensic Analyst?
<--- Score

52. What communications are necessary to support the implementation of the solution?
<--- Score

53. Are possible solutions generated and tested?
<--- Score

**54. Are your user terms of service clear and understandable?**
<--- Score

55. Risk Identification: What are the possible risk events your organization faces in relation to GIAC Certified Forensic Analyst?
<--- Score

56. What is the team's contingency plan for potential problems occurring in implementation?
<--- Score

57. For decision problems, how do you develop a decision statement?
<--- Score

**58. What documentation has been developed?**
<--- Score

59. How does the solution remove the key sources of issues discovered in the analyze phase?
<--- Score

60. Is a solution implementation plan established, including schedule/work breakdown structure, resources, risk management plan, cost/budget, and control plan?
<--- Score

61. What can you do to improve?
<--- Score

62. Who will be responsible for documenting the GIAC Certified Forensic Analyst requirements in detail?
<--- Score

63. What went well, what should change, what can improve?
<--- Score

64. Is there a high likelihood that any recommendations will achieve their intended results?
<--- Score

65. Which of the recognised risks out of all risks can be most likely transferred?
<--- Score

66. Is there a cost/benefit analysis of optimal solution(s)?
<--- Score

67. What attendant changes will need to be made to ensure that the solution is successful?
<--- Score

68. Who controls key decisions that will be made?
<--- Score

69. Are new and improved process ('should be') maps developed?
<--- Score

70. To what extent does management recognize GIAC Certified Forensic Analyst as a tool to increase the results?
<--- Score

71. What are your current levels and trends in key measures or indicators of workforce and leader development?
<--- Score

72. What practices helps your organization to develop its capacity to recognize patterns?
<--- Score

73. What is the risk?
<--- Score

74. Do those selected for the GIAC Certified Forensic Analyst team have a good general understanding of what GIAC Certified Forensic Analyst is all about?
<--- Score

75. Can you identify any significant risks or exposures to GIAC Certified Forensic Analyst third- parties (vendors, service providers, alliance partners etc) that concern you?
<--- Score

76. Are you assessing GIAC Certified Forensic Analyst and risk?
<--- Score

77. How do you measure improved GIAC Certified Forensic Analyst service perception, and satisfaction?
<--- Score

78. How do you decide how much to remunerate an employee?
<--- Score

79. Describe the design of the pilot and what tests were conducted, if any?
<--- Score

80. Is supporting GIAC Certified Forensic Analyst documentation required?
<--- Score

81. How can you improve performance?
<--- Score

82. How will you know that you have improved?
<--- Score

83. How do the GIAC Certified Forensic Analyst results compare with the performance of your competitors and other organizations with similar offerings?
<--- Score

84. How does the team improve its work?
<--- Score

85. Are improved process ('should be') maps modified based on pilot data and analysis?

<--- Score

86. Is the scope clearly documented?
<--- Score

87. How did the team generate the list of possible solutions?
<--- Score

88. How do you manage and improve your GIAC Certified Forensic Analyst work systems to deliver customer value and achieve organizational success and sustainability?
<--- Score

89. What tools were used to tap into the creativity and encourage 'outside the box' thinking?
<--- Score

90. What is the GIAC Certified Forensic Analyst's sustainability risk?
<--- Score

91. How will you measure the results?
<--- Score

92. Are the best solutions selected?
<--- Score

**93. Is litigation an effective solution?**
<--- Score

94. How will the organization know that the solution worked?
<--- Score

95. How do you define the solutions' scope?
<--- Score

96. Are risk triggers captured?
<--- Score

97. What does the 'should be' process map/design look like?
<--- Score

98. How do you go about comparing GIAC Certified Forensic Analyst approaches/solutions?
<--- Score

99. What tools were used to evaluate the potential solutions?
<--- Score

Add up total points for this section:
_ _ _ _ _ = Total points for this section

Divided by: _ _ _ _ _ _ (number of statements answered) = _ _ _ _ _ _
Average score for this section

Transfer your score to the GIAC Certified Forensic Analyst Index at the beginning of the Self-Assessment.

# CRITERION #6: CONTROL:

INTENT: Implement the practical solution. Maintain the performance and correct possible complications.

In my belief, the answer to this question is clearly defined:

5 Strongly Agree

4 Agree

3 Neutral

2 Disagree

1 Strongly Disagree

1. How might the organization capture best practices and lessons learned so as to leverage improvements across the business?
<--- Score

2. Where do ideas that reach policy makers and planners as proposals for GIAC Certified Forensic Analyst strengthening and reform actually originate?
<--- Score

3. How do you plan on providing proper recognition and disclosure of supporting companies?
<--- Score

4. Are there documented procedures?
<--- Score

5. Is a response plan in place for when the input, process, or output measures indicate an 'out-of-control' condition?
<--- Score

6. What is your theory of human motivation, and how does your compensation plan fit with that view?
<--- Score

7. How do you establish and deploy modified action plans if circumstances require a shift in plans and rapid execution of new plans?
<--- Score

8. What is the best design framework for GIAC Certified Forensic Analyst organization now that, in a post industrial-age if the top-down, command and control model is no longer relevant?
<--- Score

9. What are the critical parameters to watch?
<--- Score

10. What quality tools were useful in the control phase?
<--- Score

11. What are you attempting to measure/monitor?

<--- Score

12. What adjustments to the strategies are needed?
<--- Score

**13. How did Facebook monitor what these developers did with all the data that they collected?**
<--- Score

14. Are pertinent alerts monitored, analyzed and distributed to appropriate personnel?
<--- Score

15. What is the control/monitoring plan?
<--- Score

16. Are documented procedures clear and easy to follow for the operators?
<--- Score

17. Is there a GIAC Certified Forensic Analyst Communication plan covering who needs to get what information when?
<--- Score

18. Are the planned controls working?
<--- Score

19. Can support from partners be adjusted?
<--- Score

20. Who is the GIAC Certified Forensic Analyst process owner?
<--- Score

21. What is the recommended frequency of auditing?
<--- Score

22. Are you measuring, monitoring and predicting GIAC Certified Forensic Analyst activities to optimize operations and profitability, and enhancing outcomes?
<--- Score

23. Implementation Planning: is a pilot needed to test the changes before a full roll out occurs?
<--- Score

24. How will you measure your QA plan's effectiveness?
<--- Score

25. How likely is the current GIAC Certified Forensic Analyst plan to come in on schedule or on budget?
<--- Score

26. What other areas of the organization might benefit from the GIAC Certified Forensic Analyst team's improvements, knowledge, and learning?
<--- Score

27. How do you encourage people to take control and responsibility?
<--- Score

28. Is new knowledge gained imbedded in the response plan?
<--- Score

29. What should the next improvement project be that is related to GIAC Certified Forensic Analyst?

<--- Score

30. How will new or emerging customer needs/
requirements be checked/communicated to orient
the process toward meeting the new specifications
and continually reducing variation?
<--- Score

31. Does a troubleshooting guide exist or is it needed?
<--- Score

32. Has the improved process and its steps been
standardized?
<--- Score

33. Who controls critical resources?
<--- Score

34. Against what alternative is success being
measured?
<--- Score

35. How do you select, collect, align, and
integrate GIAC Certified Forensic Analyst data and
information for tracking daily operations and overall
organizational performance, including progress
relative to strategic objectives and action plans?
<--- Score

36. Is knowledge gained on process shared and
institutionalized?
<--- Score

37. Do you monitor the effectiveness of your GIAC
Certified Forensic Analyst activities?
<--- Score

38. What key inputs and outputs are being measured on an ongoing basis?
<--- Score

39. Is reporting being used or needed?
<--- Score

**40. Have you begun to build a response plan?**
<--- Score

**41. Do you have a communication plan ready to go after a data breach?**
<--- Score

42. Is there a recommended audit plan for routine surveillance inspections of GIAC Certified Forensic Analyst's gains?
<--- Score

43. In the case of a GIAC Certified Forensic Analyst project, the criteria for the audit derive from implementation objectives. an audit of a GIAC Certified Forensic Analyst project involves assessing whether the recommendations outlined for implementation have been met. Can you track that any GIAC Certified Forensic Analyst project is implemented as planned, and is it working?
<--- Score

44. Is there a standardized process?
<--- Score

45. Is there documentation that will support the successful operation of the improvement?
<--- Score

46. Is there a documented and implemented monitoring plan?

<--- Score

47. What should you measure to verify efficiency gains?

<--- Score

48. How will the day-to-day responsibilities for monitoring and continual improvement be transferred from the improvement team to the process owner?

<--- Score

49. How will the process owner verify improvement in present and future sigma levels, process capabilities?

<--- Score

**50. Incident Response Plans -what might work for us?**

<--- Score

51. Does the GIAC Certified Forensic Analyst performance meet the customer's requirements?

<--- Score

**52. Do you have an Incident Response Plan in place in the event of a security breach?**

<--- Score

53. What do your reports reflect?

<--- Score

**54. Is a data breach response plan in place?**

<--- Score

55. Have new or revised work instructions resulted?
<--- Score

56. Is a response plan established and deployed?
<--- Score

57. How do senior leaders actions reflect a commitment to the organizations GIAC Certified Forensic Analyst values?
<--- Score

58. How can you best use all of your knowledge repositories to enhance learning and sharing?
<--- Score

59. Does the response plan contain a definite closed loop continual improvement scheme (e.g., plan-do-check-act)?
<--- Score

60. What are the known security controls?
<--- Score

61. Is there a control plan in place for sustaining improvements (short and long-term)?
<--- Score

62. Who will be in control?
<--- Score

63. Are controls in place and consistently applied?
<--- Score

64. Are new process steps, standards, and documentation ingrained into normal operations?

<--- Score

65. Who has control over resources?
<--- Score

66. How is change control managed?
<--- Score

67. Can you adapt and adjust to changing GIAC Certified Forensic Analyst situations?
<--- Score

68. How will the process owner and team be able to hold the gains?
<--- Score

69. Act/Adjust: What Do you Need to Do Differently?
<--- Score

70. What do you stand for--and what are you against?
<--- Score

71. Is there a transfer of ownership and knowledge to process owner and process team tasked with the responsibilities.
<--- Score

72. Are operating procedures consistent?
<--- Score

73. Will the team be available to assist members in planning investigations?
<--- Score

74. How do controls support value?
<--- Score

75. How do your controls stack up?
<--- Score

76. Will your goals reflect your program budget?
<--- Score

77. How will input, process, and output variables be checked to detect for sub-optimal conditions?
<--- Score

78. How will report readings be checked to effectively monitor performance?
<--- Score

79. Do you monitor the GIAC Certified Forensic Analyst decisions made and fine tune them as they evolve?
<--- Score

80. What do you measure to verify effectiveness gains?
<--- Score

81. Will any special training be provided for results interpretation?
<--- Score

82. You may have created your quality measures at a time when you lacked resources, technology wasn't up to the required standard, or low service levels were the industry norm. Have those circumstances changed?
<--- Score

83. What other systems, operations, processes, and

infrastructures (hiring practices, staffing, training, incentives/rewards, metrics/dashboards/scorecards, etc.) need updates, additions, changes, or deletions in order to facilitate knowledge transfer and improvements?

<--- Score

84. Are suggested corrective/restorative actions indicated on the response plan for known causes to problems that might surface?

<--- Score

85. Do the GIAC Certified Forensic Analyst decisions you make today help people and the planet tomorrow?

<--- Score

86. Are the planned controls in place?

<--- Score

**87. One day; you may be the victim of a data breach and need to answer questions from customers and the press immediately. Are you ready for each possible scenario; have you decided on a communication plan that reduces the impact on your support team while giving the most accurate information to the data subjects? Who is your company spokesperson and will you be ready even if the breach becomes public out of usual office hours?**

<--- Score

88. What can you control?

<--- Score

89. Does job training on the documented procedures

need to be part of the process team's education and training?
<--- Score

90. What are the key elements of your GIAC Certified Forensic Analyst performance improvement system, including your evaluation, organizational learning, and innovation processes?
<--- Score

91. Does GIAC Certified Forensic Analyst appropriately measure and monitor risk?
<--- Score

**92. Does your plan evolve as the scenario became more clear?**
<--- Score

93. Who sets the GIAC Certified Forensic Analyst standards?
<--- Score

Add up total points for this section:
_ _ _ _ _ = Total points for this section

Divided by: _ _ _ _ _ _ (number of statements answered) = _ _ _ _ _ _
Average score for this section

Transfer your score to the GIAC Certified Forensic Analyst Index at the beginning of the Self-Assessment.

# CRITERION #7: SUSTAIN:

INTENT: Retain the benefits.

In my belief, the answer to this question is clearly defined:

5 Strongly Agree

4 Agree

3 Neutral

2 Disagree

1 Strongly Disagree

1. How do you stay inspired?
<--- Score

2. Has implementation been effective in reaching specified objectives so far?
<--- Score

3. What you are going to do to affect the numbers?
<--- Score

4. What are the short and long-term GIAC Certified

Forensic Analyst goals?
<--- Score

5. What are you challenging?
<--- Score

6. Are your responses positive or negative?
<--- Score

7. Ask yourself: how would you do this work if you only had one staff member to do it?
<--- Score

8. What management system can you use to leverage the GIAC Certified Forensic Analyst experience, ideas, and concerns of the people closest to the work to be done?
<--- Score

9. How do you make it meaningful in connecting GIAC Certified Forensic Analyst with what users do day-to-day?
<--- Score

10. Why is GIAC Certified Forensic Analyst important for you now?
<--- Score

11. Will it be accepted by users?
<--- Score

12. What does your signature ensure?
<--- Score

**13. When and where will remediation be provided?**
<--- Score

14. If you had to leave your organization for a year and the only communication you could have with employees/colleagues was a single paragraph, what would you write?
<--- Score

15. How do you engage the workforce, in addition to satisfying them?
<--- Score

16. Do you have the right capabilities and capacities?
<--- Score

17. Which GIAC Certified Forensic Analyst goals are the most important?
<--- Score

18. What is the purpose of GIAC Certified Forensic Analyst in relation to the mission?
<--- Score

**19. Who (or what) is a System Owner and what do they do?**
<--- Score

20. What business benefits will GIAC Certified Forensic Analyst goals deliver if achieved?
<--- Score

**21. What is a breach of trust?**
<--- Score

22. Who is on the team?
<--- Score

23. Who is responsible for GIAC Certified Forensic Analyst?
<--- Score

24. Why should you adopt a GIAC Certified Forensic Analyst framework?
<--- Score

25. What are the essentials of internal GIAC Certified Forensic Analyst management?
<--- Score

26. What is the craziest thing you can do?
<--- Score

27. What stupid rule would you most like to kill?
<--- Score

28. What is your question? Why?
<--- Score

29. Where can you break convention?
<--- Score

30. Do you think GIAC Certified Forensic Analyst accomplishes the goals you expect it to accomplish?
<--- Score

**31. How will you know when a compromise has been contained?**
<--- Score

32. In retrospect, of the projects that you pulled the plug on, what percent do you wish had been allowed to keep going, and what percent do you wish had ended earlier?

<--- Score

33. What is the kind of project structure that would be appropriate for your GIAC Certified Forensic Analyst project, should it be formal and complex, or can it be less formal and relatively simple?
<--- Score

34. What trouble can you get into?
<--- Score

35. How much contingency will be available in the budget?
<--- Score

36. How can you incorporate support to ensure safe and effective use of GIAC Certified Forensic Analyst into the services that you provide?
<--- Score

**37. Does it stand to reason that in all instances when damages occur that there was previously a reasonable likelihood for harm giving rise to liability for a failure to warn?**
<--- Score

38. How much does GIAC Certified Forensic Analyst help?
<--- Score

39. When you map the key players in your own work and the types/domains of relationships with them, which relationships do you find easy and which challenging, and why?
<--- Score

40. Why is it important to have senior management support for a GIAC Certified Forensic Analyst project?
<--- Score

41. What new services of functionality will be implemented next with GIAC Certified Forensic Analyst ?
<--- Score

42. Who will manage the integration of tools?
<--- Score

43. Who else should you help?
<--- Score

**44. How different would your life be without access to social media sites like Facebook?**
<--- Score

**45. What information is private?**
<--- Score

46. Were lessons learned captured and communicated?
<--- Score

47. Which models, tools and techniques are necessary?
<--- Score

48. What is the range of capabilities?
<--- Score

49. How do you keep the momentum going?
<--- Score

50. What threat is GIAC Certified Forensic Analyst addressing?

<--- Score

**51. What is the role of your organizations Information Security Officer?**

<--- Score

52. How do you deal with GIAC Certified Forensic Analyst changes?

<--- Score

**53. What are the rights and responsibilities of citizenship?**

<--- Score

**54. How do you know you have all the parts in place?**

<--- Score

55. Do you say no to customers for no reason?

<--- Score

**56. Can you go back in time to see what happened on a system?**

<--- Score

57. When information truly is ubiquitous, when reach and connectivity are completely global, when computing resources are infinite, and when a whole new set of impossibilities are not only possible, but happening, what will that do to your business?

<--- Score

**58. How did the compromise occur?**

<--- Score

59. What is the funding source for this project?
<--- Score

60. How does GIAC Certified Forensic Analyst integrate with other business initiatives?
<--- Score

61. If you do not follow, then how to lead?
<--- Score

62. Who are the key stakeholders?
<--- Score

63. How do you know if you are successful?
<--- Score

64. What are the gaps in your knowledge and experience?
<--- Score

65. In the past year, what have you done (or could you have done) to increase the accurate perception of your company/brand as ethical and honest?
<--- Score

66. Is GIAC Certified Forensic Analyst realistic, or are you setting yourself up for failure?
<--- Score

67. Who is responsible for errors?
<--- Score

68. What are specific GIAC Certified Forensic Analyst rules to follow?
<--- Score

69. What are the barriers to increased GIAC Certified Forensic Analyst production?
<--- Score

70. What would you recommend your friend do if he/she were facing this dilemma?
<--- Score

71. Why do and why don't your customers like your organization?
<--- Score

72. What is your competitive advantage?
<--- Score

73. What are the long-term GIAC Certified Forensic Analyst goals?
<--- Score

74. What happens if you do not have enough funding?
<--- Score

75. Which functions and people interact with the supplier and or customer?
<--- Score

76. Do you have an implicit bias for capital investments over people investments?
<--- Score

77. Who do you think the world wants your organization to be?
<--- Score

78. Are assumptions made in GIAC Certified Forensic Analyst stated explicitly?

<--- Score

79. What goals did you miss?

<--- Score

80. Who do you want your customers to become?

<--- Score

81. How do you manage GIAC Certified Forensic Analyst Knowledge Management (KM)?

<--- Score

82. How do you foster the skills, knowledge, talents, attributes, and characteristics you want to have?

<--- Score

83. Who is the main stakeholder, with ultimate responsibility for driving GIAC Certified Forensic Analyst forward?

<--- Score

84. Are there any disadvantages to implementing GIAC Certified Forensic Analyst? There might be some that are less obvious?

<--- Score

85. Who have you, as a company, historically been when you've been at your best?

<--- Score

86. What is your BATNA (best alternative to a negotiated agreement)?

<--- Score

**87. Do you know what normal activity in your environment looks like?**

<--- Score

**88. When should you involve law enforcement?**

<--- Score

89. Is there any reason to believe the opposite of my current belief?

<--- Score

90. Do you think you know, or do you know you know ?

<--- Score

**91. How do breaches occur?**

<--- Score

92. Marketing budgets are tighter, consumers are more skeptical, and social media has changed forever the way we talk about GIAC Certified Forensic Analyst. How do you gain traction?

<--- Score

93. How do you provide a safe environment -physically and emotionally?

<--- Score

94. What one word do you want to own in the minds of your customers, employees, and partners?

<--- Score

**95. No Sensitive Systems?**

<--- Score

96. What do we do when new problems arise?

<--- Score

97. What potential megatrends could make your business model obsolete?
<--- Score

98. Which individuals, teams or departments will be involved in GIAC Certified Forensic Analyst?
<--- Score

99. Can you maintain your growth without detracting from the factors that have contributed to your success?
<--- Score

**100. How will remediation funds be spent?**
<--- Score

101. What is your formula for success in GIAC Certified Forensic Analyst ?
<--- Score

**102. What Information Do They Want ?**
<--- Score

103. What are the potential basics of GIAC Certified Forensic Analyst fraud?
<--- Score

104. What are the top 3 things at the forefront of your GIAC Certified Forensic Analyst agendas for the next 3 years?
<--- Score

105. What are the key enablers to make this GIAC Certified Forensic Analyst move?

<--- Score

106. Did your employees make progress today?
<--- Score

**107. Should government regulate social media sites?**
<--- Score

108. How do you set GIAC Certified Forensic Analyst stretch targets and how do you get people to not only participate in setting these stretch targets but also that they strive to achieve these?
<--- Score

109. How do you go about securing GIAC Certified Forensic Analyst?
<--- Score

110. What are the usability implications of GIAC Certified Forensic Analyst actions?
<--- Score

111. How can you become the company that would put you out of business?
<--- Score

112. How will you motivate the stakeholders with the least vested interest?
<--- Score

113. What will be the consequences to the stakeholder (financial, reputation etc) if GIAC Certified Forensic Analyst does not go ahead or fails to deliver the objectives?
<--- Score

114. What current systems have to be understood and/or changed?
<--- Score

115. What are the rules and assumptions your industry operates under? What if the opposite were true?
<--- Score

116. What are the business goals GIAC Certified Forensic Analyst is aiming to achieve?
<--- Score

117. Can the schedule be done in the given time?
<--- Score

118. How do you maintain GIAC Certified Forensic Analyst's Integrity?
<--- Score

119. What is the recommended frequency of auditing?
<--- Score

120. What will drive GIAC Certified Forensic Analyst change?
<--- Score

121. If your company went out of business tomorrow, would anyone who doesn't get a paycheck here care?
<--- Score

122. Are you / should you be revolutionary or evolutionary?
<--- Score

123. Are new benefits received and understood?

<--- Score

124. How likely is it that a customer would recommend your company to a friend or colleague?
<--- Score

**125. Whats My First Move After a Breach Happens?**
<--- Score

126. Is the GIAC Certified Forensic Analyst organization completing tasks effectively and efficiently?
<--- Score

127. What GIAC Certified Forensic Analyst skills are most important?
<--- Score

128. How do customers see your organization?
<--- Score

129. Who is responsible for ensuring appropriate resources (time, people and money) are allocated to GIAC Certified Forensic Analyst?
<--- Score

130. How important is GIAC Certified Forensic Analyst to the user organizations mission?
<--- Score

131. Is there a work around that you can use?
<--- Score

**132. Which encryption methods uses AES technology?**
<--- Score

**133. Who reported the breach?**
<--- Score

134. What kind of crime could a potential new hire have committed that would not only not disqualify him/her from being hired by your organization, but would actually indicate that he/she might be a particularly good fit?
<--- Score

135. What are you trying to prove to yourself, and how might it be hijacking your life and business success?
<--- Score

136. Are you satisfied with your current role?  If not, what is missing from it?
<--- Score

**137. Could others gain or be provided access without the knowledge of your organization?**
<--- Score

138. If there were zero limitations, what would you do differently?
<--- Score

139. What happens at your organization when people fail?
<--- Score

140. How do you listen to customers to obtain actionable information?
<--- Score

141. Operational - will it work?

<--- Score

142. Are there any activities that you can take off your to do list?
<--- Score

143. Can you break it down?
<--- Score

144. What is it like to work for you?
<--- Score

145. Can you do all this work?
<--- Score

146. What are current GIAC Certified Forensic Analyst paradigms?
<--- Score

**147. Forensics are performed?**
<--- Score

**148. How does the Constitution protect freedom of expression?**
<--- Score

149. At what moment would you think; Will I get fired?
<--- Score

150. What information is critical to your organization that your executives are ignoring?
<--- Score

**151. Were there any witnesses?**
<--- Score

152. Who are four people whose careers you have enhanced?

<--- Score

153. Why not do GIAC Certified Forensic Analyst?

<--- Score

154. What would have to be true for the option on the table to be the best possible choice?

<--- Score

155. Do you have enough freaky customers in your portfolio pushing you to the limit day in and day out?

<--- Score

156. Is GIAC Certified Forensic Analyst dependent on the successful delivery of a current project?

<--- Score

157. Do you see more potential in people than they do in themselves?

<--- Score

**158. An Incident Happens: What Next?**

<--- Score

159. How do you ensure that implementations of GIAC Certified Forensic Analyst products are done in a way that ensures safety?

<--- Score

**160. Go over the scenario carefully. What do you know?**

<--- Score

161. If you were responsible for initiating and

implementing major changes in your organization, what steps might you take to ensure acceptance of those changes?

<--- Score

162. If your customer were your grandmother, would you tell her to buy what you're selling?

<--- Score

### 163. Which breaches are being litigated?

<--- Score

164. Are the assumptions believable and achievable?

<--- Score

165. Are you making progress, and are you making progress as GIAC Certified Forensic Analyst leaders?

<--- Score

166. Have new benefits been realized?

<--- Score

167. How will you know that the GIAC Certified Forensic Analyst project has been successful?

<--- Score

168. What are the challenges?

<--- Score

169. To whom do you add value?

<--- Score

170. How do you foster innovation?

<--- Score

### 171. What is your organizations Information

**Security Governance Structure?**

<--- Score

172. How will you insure seamless interoperability of GIAC Certified Forensic Analyst moving forward?

<--- Score

173. Are you maintaining a past–present–future perspective throughout the GIAC Certified Forensic Analyst discussion?

<--- Score

174. What knowledge, skills and characteristics mark a good GIAC Certified Forensic Analyst project manager?

<--- Score

175. What are your most important goals for the strategic GIAC Certified Forensic Analyst objectives?

<--- Score

176. Why should people listen to you?

<--- Score

177. How do you accomplish your long range GIAC Certified Forensic Analyst goals?

<--- Score

**178. How should you prepare to enable a prompt reaction to a potential breach?**

<--- Score

179. Is the impact that GIAC Certified Forensic Analyst has shown?

<--- Score

180. How do you govern and fulfill your societal responsibilities?

<--- Score

181. What unique value proposition (UVP) do you offer?

<--- Score

182. How do you track customer value, profitability or financial return, organizational success, and sustainability?

<--- Score

183. What projects are going on in the organization today, and what resources are those projects using from the resource pools?

<--- Score

184. What role does communication play in the success or failure of a GIAC Certified Forensic Analyst project?

<--- Score

185. Are you using a design thinking approach and integrating Innovation, GIAC Certified Forensic Analyst Experience, and Brand Value?

<--- Score

186. Who will determine interim and final deadlines?

<--- Score

187. Are all key stakeholders present at all Structured Walkthroughs?

<--- Score

188. What are internal and external GIAC Certified

Forensic Analyst relations?

<--- Score

189. How do you transition from the baseline to the target?

<--- Score

190. Do you know what you are doing? And who do you call if you don't?

<--- Score

191. What may be the consequences for the performance of an organization if all stakeholders are not consulted regarding GIAC Certified Forensic Analyst?

<--- Score

192. If you weren't already in this business, would you enter it today? And if not, what are you going to do about it?

<--- Score

193. Are you paying enough attention to the partners your company depends on to succeed?

<--- Score

**194. When did the breach take place?**

<--- Score

195. Who will be responsible for deciding whether GIAC Certified Forensic Analyst goes ahead or not after the initial investigations?

<--- Score

196. Instead of going to current contacts for new ideas, what if you reconnected with dormant

contacts--the people you used to know? If you were going reactivate a dormant tie, who would it be?
<--- Score

197. What must you excel at?
<--- Score

198. Is your basic point _____ or _____?
<--- Score

199. What happens when a new employee joins the organization?
<--- Score

200. How do you proactively clarify deliverables and GIAC Certified Forensic Analyst quality expectations?
<--- Score

201. How is implementation research currently incorporated into each of your goals?
<--- Score

202. Is maximizing GIAC Certified Forensic Analyst protection the same as minimizing GIAC Certified Forensic Analyst loss?
<--- Score

203. How do you assess the GIAC Certified Forensic Analyst pitfalls that are inherent in implementing it?
<--- Score

204. Do GIAC Certified Forensic Analyst rules make a reasonable demand on a users capabilities?
<--- Score

205. What should you stop doing?

<--- Score

206. How do you keep records, of what?
<--- Score

207. Why will customers want to buy your organizations products/services?
<--- Score

208. Whose voice (department, ethnic group, women, older workers, etc) might you have missed hearing from in your company, and how might you amplify this voice to create positive momentum for your business?
<--- Score

209. Are you relevant? Will you be relevant five years from now? Ten?
<--- Score

210. What did you miss in the interview for the worst hire you ever made?
<--- Score

211. Have benefits been optimized with all key stakeholders?
<--- Score

212. How can you negotiate GIAC Certified Forensic Analyst successfully with a stubborn boss, an irate client, or a deceitful coworker?
<--- Score

213. How can you become more high-tech but still be high touch?
<--- Score

214. Who, on the executive team or the board, has spoken to a customer recently?
<--- Score

215. Do you have past GIAC Certified Forensic Analyst successes?
<--- Score

216. What is an unauthorized commitment?
<--- Score

217. What is effective GIAC Certified Forensic Analyst?
<--- Score

218. What have you done to protect your business from competitive encroachment?
<--- Score

219. Are the criteria for selecting recommendations stated?
<--- Score

220. In a project to restructure GIAC Certified Forensic Analyst outcomes, which stakeholders would you involve?
<--- Score

221. Will there be any necessary staff changes (redundancies or new hires)?
<--- Score

222. How long will it take to change?
<--- Score

223. Who uses your product in ways you never

expected?

<--- Score

224. Would you rather sell to knowledgeable and informed customers or to uninformed customers?

<--- Score

225. What are strategies for increasing support and reducing opposition?

<--- Score

226. How do you determine the key elements that affect GIAC Certified Forensic Analyst workforce satisfaction, how are these elements determined for different workforce groups and segments?

<--- Score

227. How will you ensure you get what you expected?

<--- Score

228. Is it economical; do you have the time and money?

<--- Score

229. What was the last experiment you ran?

<--- Score

230. What is something you believe that nearly no one agrees with you on?

<--- Score

231. How do you lead with GIAC Certified Forensic Analyst in mind?

<--- Score

**232. Deprovisioning of user accounts done?**

<--- Score

233. Think of your GIAC Certified Forensic Analyst project, what are the main functions?
<--- Score

234. Are you changing as fast as the world around you?
<--- Score

235. What is a feasible sequencing of reform initiatives over time?
<--- Score

**236. How do you ensure that once employees leave your organization, they no longer have access?**
<--- Score

**237. If a breach was employee related, what is the status of the employee (terminated, still employed, arrested)?**
<--- Score

238. Who do we want your customers to become?
<--- Score

239. Who will provide the final approval of GIAC Certified Forensic Analyst deliverables?
<--- Score

240. Who are your customers?
<--- Score

241. Whom among your colleagues do you trust, and for what?

<--- Score

242. What counts that you are not counting?
<--- Score

243. If you got fired and a new hire took your place, what would she do different?
<--- Score

244. What are the success criteria that will indicate that GIAC Certified Forensic Analyst objectives have been met and the benefits delivered?
<--- Score

245. Do you feel that more should be done in the GIAC Certified Forensic Analyst area?
<--- Score

246. Is a GIAC Certified Forensic Analyst team work effort in place?
<--- Score

247. What are your personal philosophies regarding GIAC Certified Forensic Analyst and how do they influence your work?
<--- Score

248. Political -is anyone trying to undermine this project?
<--- Score

249. What have been your experiences in defining long range GIAC Certified Forensic Analyst goals?
<--- Score

250. Do you have the right people on the bus?

<--- Score

251. What relationships among GIAC Certified Forensic Analyst trends do you perceive?
<--- Score

252. How do you create buy-in?
<--- Score

253. What trophy do you want on your mantle?
<--- Score

254. How do you cross-sell and up-sell your GIAC Certified Forensic Analyst success?
<--- Score

255. If no one would ever find out about your accomplishments, how would you lead differently?
<--- Score

**256. Are any other locations/affiliated companies effected?**
<--- Score

257. How are you doing compared to your industry?
<--- Score

**258. Does the fact that a breach includes SSNs change the way you respond?**
<--- Score

**259. Admissible in court?**
<--- Score

**260. Which breaches will be litigated?**
<--- Score

261. What GIAC Certified Forensic Analyst modifications can you make work for you?
<--- Score

262. What is the source of the strategies for GIAC Certified Forensic Analyst strengthening and reform?
<--- Score

263. What is the estimated value of the project?
<--- Score

**264. What are some pros and cons about receiving personally catered advertisements?**
<--- Score

Add up total points for this section:
_____ = Total points for this section

Divided by: _____ (number of statements answered) = _____ Average score for this section

Transfer your score to the GIAC Certified Forensic Analyst Index at the beginning of the Self-Assessment.

# GIAC Certified Forensic Analyst and Managing Projects, Criteria for Project Managers:

# 1.0 Initiating Process Group: GIAC Certified Forensic Analyst

1. What communication items need improvement?

2. What were things that you did very well and want to do the same again on the next GIAC Certified Forensic Analyst project?

3. Are identified risks being monitored properly, are new risks arising during the GIAC Certified Forensic Analyst project or are foreseen risks occurring?

4. What were things that you need to improve?

5. What is the NEXT thing to do?

6. During which stage of Risk planning are modeling techniques used to determine overall effects of risks on GIAC Certified Forensic Analyst project objectives for high probability, high impact risks?

7. If action is called for, what form should it take?

8. Have you evaluated the teams performance and asked for feedback?

9. When will the GIAC Certified Forensic Analyst project be done?

10. What areas were overlooked on this GIAC Certified Forensic Analyst project?

11. Did the GIAC Certified Forensic Analyst project team have the right skills?

12. The GIAC Certified Forensic Analyst project you are managing has nine stakeholders. How many channel of communications are there between corresponding stakeholders?

13. Based on your GIAC Certified Forensic Analyst project communication management plan, what worked well?

14. What do you need to do?

15. Measurable - are the targets measurable?

16. Who is funding the GIAC Certified Forensic Analyst project?

17. Do you know all the stakeholders impacted by the GIAC Certified Forensic Analyst project and what needs are?

18. Where must it be done?

19. When must it be done?

20. Who is behind the GIAC Certified Forensic Analyst project?

# 1.1 Project Charter: GIAC Certified Forensic Analyst

21. GIAC Certified Forensic Analyst project background: what is the primary motivation for this GIAC Certified Forensic Analyst project?

22. How will you know a change is an improvement?

23. Why do you need to manage scope?

24. Are there special technology requirements?

25. Customer: who are you doing the GIAC Certified Forensic Analyst project for?

26. How will you learn more about the process or system you are trying to improve?

27. How do you manage integration?

28. Did your GIAC Certified Forensic Analyst project ask for this?

29. Market – identify products market, including whether it is outside of the objective: what is the purpose of the program or GIAC Certified Forensic Analyst project?

30. Success determination factors: how will the success of the GIAC Certified Forensic Analyst project be determined from the customers perspective?

31. Are you building in-house ?

32. For whom?

33. Environmental stewardship and sustainability considerations: what is the process that will be used to ensure compliance with the environmental stewardship policy?

34. Assumptions: what factors, for planning purposes, are you considering to be true?

35. What are some examples of a business case?

36. What is the business need?

37. What date will the task finish?

38. Who is the GIAC Certified Forensic Analyst project Manager?

39. Why have you chosen the aim you have set forth?

40. Assumptions and constraints: what assumptions were made in defining the GIAC Certified Forensic Analyst project?

# 1.2 Stakeholder Register: GIAC Certified Forensic Analyst

41. How much influence do they have on the GIAC Certified Forensic Analyst project?

42. What opportunities exist to provide communications?

43. Who wants to talk about Security?

44. Who are the stakeholders?

45. What are the major GIAC Certified Forensic Analyst project milestones requiring communications or providing communications opportunities?

46. Is your organization ready for change?

47. How will reports be created?

48. What & Why?

49. What is the power of the stakeholder?

50. How big is the gap?

51. How should employers make voices heard?

52. Who is managing stakeholder engagement?

# 1.3 Stakeholder Analysis Matrix: GIAC Certified Forensic Analyst

53. Who will obstruct/hinder the GIAC Certified Forensic Analyst project if they are not involved?

54. Who are potential allies and opponents?

55. Who has not been involved up to now and should have been?

56. Organizational Applicability?

57. How are the threatened GIAC Certified Forensic Analyst project targets being used?

58. Identify the stakeholders levels most frequently used –or at least sought– in your GIAC Certified Forensic Analyst projects and for which purpose?

59. What is the stakeholders power and status in relation to the GIAC Certified Forensic Analyst project?

60. How to measure the achievement of the Outputs?

61. Tactics: eg, surprise, major contracts?

62. What can the GIAC Certified Forensic Analyst projects outcome be used for?

63. What do people from other organizations see as your organizations weaknesses?

64. Price, value, quality?

65. Experience, knowledge, data?

66. Do recommendations include actions to address any differential distribution of impacts?

67. What is the relationship among stakeholders?

68. Who holds positions of responsibility in interested organizations?

69. Continuity, supply chain robustness?

70. How do rules, behaviors affect stakes?

71. Why do you care?

72. Vital contracts and partners?

## 2.0 Planning Process Group: GIAC Certified Forensic Analyst

73. On which process should team members spend the most time?

74. Are there efficient coordination mechanisms to avoid overloading the counterparts, participating stakeholders?

75. In what way has the program contributed towards the issue culture and development included on the public agenda?

76. Is the pace of implementing the products of the program ensuring the completeness of the results of the GIAC Certified Forensic Analyst project?

77. When will the GIAC Certified Forensic Analyst project be done?

78. GIAC Certified Forensic Analyst project assessment; why did you do this GIAC Certified Forensic Analyst project?

79. Does the program have follow-up mechanisms (to verify the quality of the products, punctuality of delivery, etc.) to measure progress in the achievement of the envisaged results?

80. How does activity resource estimation affect activity duration estimation?

81. Are the follow-up indicators relevant and do they meet the quality needed to measure the outputs and outcomes of the GIAC Certified Forensic Analyst project?

82. Why is it important to determine activity sequencing on GIAC Certified Forensic Analyst projects?

83. What are the different approaches to building the WBS?

84. Did you read it correctly?

85. Product breakdown structure (pbs): what is the GIAC Certified Forensic Analyst project result or product, and how should it look like, what are its parts?

86. Mitigate. what will you do to minimize the impact should a risk event occur?

87. How well will the chosen processes produce the expected results?

88. You did your readings, yes?

89. What types of differentiated effects are resulting from the GIAC Certified Forensic Analyst project and to what extent?

90. Are the necessary foundations in place to ensure the sustainability of the results of the GIAC Certified Forensic Analyst project?

91. To what extent are the participating departments

coordinating with each other?

92. Just how important is your work to the overall success of the GIAC Certified Forensic Analyst project?

# 2.1 Project Management Plan: GIAC Certified Forensic Analyst

93. Will you add a schedule and diagram?

94. What is the justification?

95. Is mitigation authorized or recommended?

96. What are the assumptions?

97. How do you manage time?

98. What data/reports/tools/etc. do program managers need?

99. What if, for example, the positive direction and vision of your organization causes expected trends to change resulting in greater need than expected?

100. Are the proposed GIAC Certified Forensic Analyst project purposes different than a previously authorized GIAC Certified Forensic Analyst project?

101. Are comparable cost estimates used for comparing, screening and selecting alternative plans, and has a reasonable cost estimate been developed for the recommended plan?

102. What is GIAC Certified Forensic Analyst project scope management?

103. Is the budget realistic?

104. How well are you able to manage your risk?

105. When is the GIAC Certified Forensic Analyst project management plan created?

106. What are the deliverables?

107. Has the selected plan been formulated using cost effectiveness and incremental analysis techniques?

108. Are there any windfall benefits that would accrue to the GIAC Certified Forensic Analyst project sponsor or other parties?

109. What went right?

110. Is there an incremental analysis/cost effectiveness analysis of proposed mitigation features based on an approved method and using an accepted model?

111. Who is the sponsor?

112. Does the implementation plan have an appropriate division of responsibilities?

## 2.2 Scope Management Plan: GIAC Certified Forensic Analyst

113. Is quality monitored from the perspective of the customers needs and expectations?

114. Who is doing what for whom?

115. Alignment to strategic goals & objectives?

116. Are vendor invoices audited for accuracy before payment?

117. Has the scope management document been updated and distributed to help prevent scope creep?

118. Is there an on-going process in place to monitor GIAC Certified Forensic Analyst project risks?

119. Are meeting objectives identified for each meeting?

120. Does the GIAC Certified Forensic Analyst project have a Quality Culture?

121. Have GIAC Certified Forensic Analyst project management standards and procedures been identified / established and documented?

122. How many changes are you making?

123. Are agendas created for each meeting with meeting objectives, meeting topics, invitee list, and

action items from past meetings?

124. Where do scope processes fit in?

125. Were GIAC Certified Forensic Analyst project team members involved in the development of activity & task decomposition?

126. Are decisions captured in a decisions log?

127. Are the proposed GIAC Certified Forensic Analyst project purposes different than the previously authorized GIAC Certified Forensic Analyst project?

128. Are actuals compared against estimates to analyze and correct variances?

129. Are issues raised, assessed, actioned, and resolved in a timely and efficient manner?

130. Is the communication plan being followed?

131. Has your organization done similar tasks before?

132. Is the quality assurance team identified?

## 2.3 Requirements Management Plan: GIAC Certified Forensic Analyst

133. What information regarding the GIAC Certified Forensic Analyst project requirements will be reported?

134. Will you perform a Requirements Risk assessment and develop a plan to deal with risks?

135. Do you have an agreed upon process for alerting the GIAC Certified Forensic Analyst project Manager if a request for change in requirements leads to a product scope change?

136. Who will do the reporting and to whom will reports be delivered?

137. Is the change control process documented?

138. Did you avoid subjective, flowery or non-specific statements?

139. Are all the stakeholders ready for the transition into the user community?

140. What is a problem?

141. Do you know which stakeholders will participate in the requirements effort?

142. How will bidders price evaluations be done, by deliverables, phases, or in a big bang?

143. How will unresolved questions be handled once approval has been obtained?

144. Did you use declarative statements?

145. What went wrong?

146. Did you distinguish the scope of work the contractor(s) will be required to do?

147. Is the system software (non-operating system) new to the IT GIAC Certified Forensic Analyst project team?

148. Could inaccurate or incomplete requirements in this GIAC Certified Forensic Analyst project create a serious risk for the business?

149. When and how will a requirements baseline be established in this GIAC Certified Forensic Analyst project?

150. Business analysis scope?

151. How often will the reporting occur?

# 2.4 Requirements Documentation: GIAC Certified Forensic Analyst

152. Do technical resources exist?

153. Is your business case still valid?

154. How does the proposed GIAC Certified Forensic Analyst project contribute to the overall objectives of your organization?

155. Do your constraints stand?

156. What facilities must be supported by the system?

157. Are there legal issues?

158. What is the risk associated with the technology?

159. What marketing channels do you want to use: e-mail, letter or sms?

160. What happens when requirements are wrong?

161. How can you document system requirements?

162. Can you check system requirements?

163. Have the benefits identified with the system being identified clearly?

164. Has requirements gathering uncovered information that would necessitate changes?

165. The problem with gathering requirements is right there in the word gathering. What images does it conjure?

166. What is your Elevator Speech?

167. What can tools do for us?

168. How linear / iterative is your Requirements Gathering process (or will it be)?

169. How will they be documented / shared?

170. Where do system and software requirements come from, what are sources?

171. If applicable; are there issues linked with the fact that this is an offshore GIAC Certified Forensic Analyst project?

## 2.5 Requirements Traceability Matrix: GIAC Certified Forensic Analyst

172. What percentage of GIAC Certified Forensic Analyst projects are producing traceability matrices between requirements and other work products?

173. Do you have a clear understanding of all subcontracts in place?

174. What is the WBS?

175. How will it affect the stakeholders personally in their career?

176. Why use a WBS?

177. How small is small enough?

178. How do you manage scope?

179. What are the chronologies, contingencies, consequences, criteria?

180. Will you use a Requirements Traceability Matrix?

181. Describe the process for approving requirements so they can be added to the traceability matrix and GIAC Certified Forensic Analyst project work can be performed. Will the GIAC Certified Forensic Analyst project requirements become approved in writing?

182. Is there a requirements traceability process in

place?

**183. Why do you manage scope?**

# 2.6 Project Scope Statement: GIAC Certified Forensic Analyst

184. What are the defined meeting materials?

185. Change management vs. change leadership - what is the difference?

186. What are the major deliverables of the GIAC Certified Forensic Analyst project?

187. Has a method and process for requirement tracking been developed?

188. Is an issue management process documented and filed?

189. Has everyone approved the GIAC Certified Forensic Analyst projects scope statement?

190. Are there adequate GIAC Certified Forensic Analyst project control systems?

191. Does the scope statement still need some clarity?

192. Is your organization structure appropriate for the GIAC Certified Forensic Analyst projects size and complexity?

193. Are there issues that could affect the existing requirements for the result, service, or product if the scope changes?

194. If there is an independent oversight contractor, have they signed off on the GIAC Certified Forensic Analyst project Plan?

195. What should you drop in order to add something new?

196. Any new risks introduced or old risks impacted. Are there issues that could affect the existing requirements for the result, service, or product if the scope changes?

197. What are the possible consequences should a risk come to occur?

198. Is there an information system for the GIAC Certified Forensic Analyst project?

199. If you were to write a list of what should not be included in the scope statement, what are the things that you would recommend be described as out-of-scope?

200. Once its defined, what is the stability of the GIAC Certified Forensic Analyst project scope?

201. Have you been able to thoroughly document the GIAC Certified Forensic Analyst projects assumptions and constraints?

202. If there are vendors, have they signed off on the GIAC Certified Forensic Analyst project Plan?

# 2.7 Assumption and Constraint Log: GIAC Certified Forensic Analyst

203. Are best practices and metrics employed to identify issues, progress, performance, etc.?

204. Are you meeting your customers expectations consistently?

205. Do documented requirements exist for all critical components and areas, including technical, business, interfaces, performance, security and conversion requirements?

206. Have adequate resources been provided by management to ensure GIAC Certified Forensic Analyst project success?

207. Is this process still needed?

208. How many GIAC Certified Forensic Analyst project staff does this specific process affect?

209. Contradictory information between different documents?

210. Diagrams and tables are included to account for complex concepts and increase overall readability?

211. Are there standards for code development?

212. Do you know what your customers expectations are regarding this process?

213. Should factors be unpredictable over time?

214. Are there ways to reduce the time it takes to get something approved?

215. Does the document/deliverable meet all requirements (for example, statement of work) specific to this deliverable?

216. Have the scope, objectives, costs, benefits and impacts been communicated to all involved and/or impacted stakeholders and work groups?

217. Are there processes in place to ensure internal consistency between the source code components?

218. Have GIAC Certified Forensic Analyst project management standards and procedures been established and documented?

219. Are formal code reviews conducted?

220. Is there adequate stakeholder participation for the vetting of requirements definition, changes and management?

221. What strengths do you have?

222. Has the approach and development strategy of the GIAC Certified Forensic Analyst project been defined, documented and accepted by the appropriate stakeholders?

## 2.8 Work Breakdown Structure: GIAC Certified Forensic Analyst

223. How much detail?

224. Is the work breakdown structure (wbs) defined and is the scope of the GIAC Certified Forensic Analyst project clear with assigned deliverable owners?

225. How will you and your GIAC Certified Forensic Analyst project team define the GIAC Certified Forensic Analyst projects scope and work breakdown structure?

226. Who has to do it?

227. How many levels?

228. What is the probability that the GIAC Certified Forensic Analyst project duration will exceed xx weeks?

229. Can you make it?

230. How far down?

231. How big is a work-package?

232. When would you develop a Work Breakdown Structure?

233. Why would you develop a Work Breakdown Structure?

234. When do you stop?

235. Is it still viable?

236. Do you need another level?

237. Where does it take place?

238. When does it have to be done?

239. Why is it useful?

240. What is the probability of completing the GIAC Certified Forensic Analyst project in less that xx days?

241. Is it a change in scope?

242. What has to be done?

# 2.9 WBS Dictionary: GIAC Certified Forensic Analyst

243. Are records maintained to show how undistributed budgets are controlled?

244. Are the wbs and organizational levels for application of the GIAC Certified Forensic Analyst projected overhead costs identified?

245. Does the contractors system provide unit or lot costs when applicable?

246. Are authorized changes being incorporated in a timely manner?

247. Are retroactive changes to direct costs and indirect costs prohibited except for the correction of errors and routine accounting adjustments?

248. Are records maintained to show full accountability for all material purchased for the contract, including the residual inventory?

249. Is undistributed budget limited to contract effort which cannot yet be planned to CWBS elements at or below the level specified for reporting to the Government?

250. Where engineering standards or other internal work measurement systems are used, is there a formal relationship between corresponding values and work package budgets?

251. Does the contractors system identify work accomplishment against the schedule plan?

252. Is subcontracted work defined and identified to the appropriate subcontractor within the proper WBS element?

253. Are detailed work packages planned as far in advance as practicable?

254. Where learning is used in developing underlying budgets is there a direct relationship between anticipated learning and time phased budgets?

255. Is data disseminated to the contractors management timely, accurate, and usable?

256. Are current budgets resulting from changes to the authorized work and/or internal replanning, reconcilable to original budgets for specified reporting items?

257. Performance to date and material commitment?

258. What are you counting on?

259. Is all budget available as management reserve identified and excluded from the performance measurement baseline?

260. Is the work done on a work package level as described in the WBS dictionary?

261. Incurrence of actual indirect costs in excess of budgets, by element of expense?

## 2.10 Schedule Management Plan: GIAC Certified Forensic Analyst

262. Does the time GIAC Certified Forensic Analyst projection include an amount for contingencies (time reserves)?

263. Must the GIAC Certified Forensic Analyst project be complete by a specified date?

264. Will the GIAC Certified Forensic Analyst project sponsor be involved in preliminary schedule reviews?

265. Were GIAC Certified Forensic Analyst project team members involved in detailed estimating and scheduling?

266. Are the people assigned to the GIAC Certified Forensic Analyst project sufficiently qualified?

267. Have GIAC Certified Forensic Analyst project management standards and procedures been identified / established and documented?

268. Who is responsible for estimating the activity durations?

269. Has the GIAC Certified Forensic Analyst project manager been identified?

270. What happens if a warning is triggered?

271. Has the GIAC Certified Forensic Analyst project

scope been baselined?

272. Are adequate resources provided for the quality assurance function?

273. How are GIAC Certified Forensic Analyst projects different from operations?

274. Have external dependencies been captured in the schedule?

275. Have GIAC Certified Forensic Analyst project team accountabilities & responsibilities been clearly defined?

276. Was the scope definition used in task sequencing?

277. What tools and techniques will be used to estimate activity durations?

278. Do all stakeholders know how to access this repository and where to find the GIAC Certified Forensic Analyst project documentation?

279. Were the budget estimates reasonable?

280. Are the appropriate IT resources adequate to meet planned commitments?

281. Is a process for scheduling and reporting defined, including forms and formats?

## 2.11 Activity List: GIAC Certified Forensic Analyst

282. The wbs is developed as part of a joint planning session. and how do you know that youhave done this right?

283. How do you determine the late start (LS) for each activity?

284. Are the required resources available or need to be acquired?

285. What will be performed?

286. In what sequence?

287. How should ongoing costs be monitored to try to keep the GIAC Certified Forensic Analyst project within budget?

288. How will it be performed?

289. When do the individual activities need to start and finish?

290. Is infrastructure setup part of your GIAC Certified Forensic Analyst project?

291. How can the GIAC Certified Forensic Analyst project be displayed graphically to better visualize the activities?

292. How detailed should a GIAC Certified Forensic Analyst project get?

293. What are the critical bottleneck activities?

294. What went well?

295. What is the LF and LS for each activity?

296. Is there anything planned that does not need to be here?

297. Can you determine the activity that must finish, before this activity can start?

298. Who will perform the work?

299. What is the total time required to complete the GIAC Certified Forensic Analyst project if no delays occur?

# 2.12 Activity Attributes: GIAC Certified Forensic Analyst

300. Activity: what is Missing?

301. Activity: fair or not fair?

302. What conclusions/generalizations can you draw from this?

303. Why?

304. Were there other ways you could have organized the data to achieve similar results?

305. What is the general pattern here?

306. How many resources do you need to complete the work scope within a limit of X number of days?

307. How difficult will it be to complete specific activities on this GIAC Certified Forensic Analyst project?

308. What is your organizations history in doing similar activities?

309. Have you identified the Activity Leveling Priority code value on each activity?

310. Is there a trend during the year?

311. How much activity detail is required?

312. Can more resources be added?

313. Do you feel very comfortable with your prediction?

314. Activity: what is In the Bag?

315. Where else does it apply?

## 2.13 Milestone List: GIAC Certified Forensic Analyst

316. Describe the concept of the technology, product or service that will be or has been developed. How will it be used?

317. Who will manage the GIAC Certified Forensic Analyst project on a day-to-day basis?

318. Sustainable financial backing?

319. New USPs?

320. Obstacles faced?

321. Identify critical paths (one or more) and which activities are on the critical path?

322. Insurmountable weaknesses?

323. Usps (unique selling points)?

324. How will the milestone be verified?

325. Do you foresee any technical risks or developmental challenges?

326. Level of the Innovation?

327. Loss of key staff?

328. How late can each activity be finished and

started?

329. What specific improvements did you make to the GIAC Certified Forensic Analyst project proposal since the previous time?

330. How soon can the activity finish?

331. Environmental effects?

332. Reliability of data, plan predictability?

333. Describe your organizations strengths and core competencies. What factors will make your organization succeed?

## 2.14 Network Diagram: GIAC Certified Forensic Analyst

334. What job or jobs precede it?

335. What must be completed before an activity can be started?

336. What is the probability of completing the GIAC Certified Forensic Analyst project in less that xx days?

337. Will crashing x weeks return more in benefits than it costs?

338. Exercise: what is the probability that the GIAC Certified Forensic Analyst project duration will exceed xx weeks?

339. What activity must be completed immediately before this activity can start?

340. Can you calculate the confidence level?

341. If a current contract exists, can you provide the vendor name, contract start, and contract expiration date?

342. If the GIAC Certified Forensic Analyst project network diagram cannot change and you have extra personnel resources, what is the BEST thing to do?

343. What controls the start and finish of a job?

344. How confident can you be in your milestone dates and the delivery date?

345. What activities must occur simultaneously with this activity?

346. Why must you schedule milestones, such as reviews, throughout the GIAC Certified Forensic Analyst project?

347. What are the Key Success Factors?

348. What is the lowest cost to complete this GIAC Certified Forensic Analyst project in xx weeks?

349. What to do and When?

350. Planning: who, how long, what to do?

351. Are the gantt chart and/or network diagram updated periodically and used to assess the overall GIAC Certified Forensic Analyst project timetable?

352. What is the completion time?

## 2.15 Activity Resource Requirements: GIAC Certified Forensic Analyst

353. When does monitoring begin?

354. Anything else?

355. What is the Work Plan Standard?

356. Time for overtime?

357. Do you use tools like decomposition and rolling-wave planning to produce the activity list and other outputs?

358. Why do you do that?

359. Other support in specific areas?

360. How many signatures do you require on a check and does this match what is in your policy and procedures?

361. How do you handle petty cash?

362. Are there unresolved issues that need to be addressed?

363. What are constraints that you might find during the Human Resource Planning process?

364. Which logical relationship does the PDM use most often?

## 2.16 Resource Breakdown Structure: GIAC Certified Forensic Analyst

365. What is each stakeholders desired outcome for the GIAC Certified Forensic Analyst project?

366. Why do you do it?

367. Changes based on input from stakeholders?

368. What defines a successful GIAC Certified Forensic Analyst project?

369. Goals for the GIAC Certified Forensic Analyst project. What is each stakeholders desired outcome for the GIAC Certified Forensic Analyst project?

370. What is the number one predictor of a groups productivity?

371. Why is this important?

372. Who needs what information?

373. How should the information be delivered?

374. Is predictive resource analysis being done?

375. What is GIAC Certified Forensic Analyst project communication management?

376. Which resource planning tool provides information on resource responsibility and

accountability?

377. The list could probably go on, but, the thing that you would most like to know is, How long & How much?

378. What is the difference between % Complete and % work?

379. When do they need the information?

380. What is the purpose of assigning and documenting responsibility?

## 2.17 Activity Duration Estimates: GIAC Certified Forensic Analyst

381. Are GIAC Certified Forensic Analyst project results verified and GIAC Certified Forensic Analyst project documents archived?

382. Are risks that are likely to affect the GIAC Certified Forensic Analyst project identified and documented?

383. GIAC Certified Forensic Analyst project manager has received activity duration estimates from his team. Which does one need in order to complete schedule development?

384. How does poking fun at technical professionals communications skills impact the industry and educational programs?

385. Which is correct?

386. What are the main types of goods and services being outsourced?

387. What functions does this software provide that cannot be done easily using other tools such as a spreadsheet or database?

388. Can they use the already stated?

389. Who will provide inputs for it?

390. Given your research into similar classes and the

work you think is required for this GIAC Certified Forensic Analyst project, what assumptions, variables, or costs would you change from the information provided above?

391. Research risk management software. Are many products available?

392. What is the BEST thing for the GIAC Certified Forensic Analyst project manager to do?

393. Why is there a growing trend in outsourcing, especially in the government?

394. What tasks must follow this task?

395. Briefly summarize the work done by Maslow, Herzberg, McClellan, McGregor, Ouchi, Thamhain and Wilemon, and Covey. How do theories relate to GIAC Certified Forensic Analyst project management?

396. How much time is required to develop it?

397. Will it help in finding or retaining employees?

398. Describe a GIAC Certified Forensic Analyst project that suffered from scope creep. Could it have been avoided?

399. What tasks can take place concurrently?

400. How do functionality, system outputs, performance, reliability, and maintainability requirements affect quality planning?

# 2.18 Duration Estimating Worksheet: GIAC Certified Forensic Analyst

401. How can the GIAC Certified Forensic Analyst project be displayed graphically to better visualize the activities?

402. Science = process: remember the scientific method?

403. When, then?

404. Define the work as completely as possible. What work will be included in the GIAC Certified Forensic Analyst project?

405. Will the GIAC Certified Forensic Analyst project collaborate with the local community and leverage resources?

406. What is next?

407. Why estimate time and cost?

408. Is the GIAC Certified Forensic Analyst project responsive to community need?

409. What utility impacts are there?

410. Small or large GIAC Certified Forensic Analyst project?

411. What is cost and GIAC Certified Forensic Analyst

project cost management?

412. Done before proceeding with this activity or what can be done concurrently?

413. What info is needed?

414. What is your role?

415. For other activities, how much delay can be tolerated?

416. What work will be included in the GIAC Certified Forensic Analyst project?

417. What questions do you have?

418. What is the total time required to complete the GIAC Certified Forensic Analyst project if no delays occur?

419. Does the GIAC Certified Forensic Analyst project provide innovative ways for stakeholders to overcome obstacles or deliver better outcomes?

## 2.19 Project Schedule: GIAC Certified Forensic Analyst

420. What is risk?

421. Why or why not?

422. Should you include sub-activities?

423. How detailed should a GIAC Certified Forensic Analyst project get?

424. How can you minimize or control changes to GIAC Certified Forensic Analyst project schedules?

425. What is GIAC Certified Forensic Analyst project management?

426. It allows the GIAC Certified Forensic Analyst project to be delivered on schedule. How Do you Use Schedules?

427. Month GIAC Certified Forensic Analyst project take?

428. Why do you need schedules?

429. How can you address that situation?

430. How closely did the initial GIAC Certified Forensic Analyst project Schedule compare with the actual schedule?

431. Are procedures defined by which the GIAC Certified Forensic Analyst project schedule may be changed?

432. Are key risk mitigation strategies added to the GIAC Certified Forensic Analyst project schedule?

433. Does the condition or event threaten the GIAC Certified Forensic Analyst projects objectives in any ways?

434. What is the difference?

435. Why do you think schedule issues often cause the most conflicts on GIAC Certified Forensic Analyst projects?

436. Did the final product meet or exceed user expectations?

437. Is there a Schedule Management Plan that establishes the criteria and activities for developing, monitoring and controlling the GIAC Certified Forensic Analyst project schedule?

438. How can slack be negative?

## 2.20 Cost Management Plan: GIAC Certified Forensic Analyst

439. Designated small business reserve?

440. Are changes in deliverable commitments agreed to by all affected groups & individuals?

441. Are all key components of a Quality Assurance Plan present?

442. The definition of the GIAC Certified Forensic Analyst project scope what needs to be accomplished?

443. Is there an onboarding process in place?

444. Are estimating assumptions and constraints captured?

445. What are the GIAC Certified Forensic Analyst project objectives?

446. What is an Acceptance Management Process?

447. Was your organizations estimating methodology being used and followed?

448. Who will prepare the cost estimates?

449. Schedule contingency – how will the schedule contingency be administrated?

450. Is it standard practice to formally commit stakeholders to the GIAC Certified Forensic Analyst project via agreements?

451. Is it a GIAC Certified Forensic Analyst project?

452. Has the business need been clearly defined?

453. How does the proposed individual meet each requirement?

454. Is it possible to track all classes of GIAC Certified Forensic Analyst project work (e.g. scheduled, un-scheduled, defect repair, etc.)?

## 2.21 Activity Cost Estimates: GIAC Certified Forensic Analyst

455. What areas does the group agree are the biggest success on the GIAC Certified Forensic Analyst project?

456. Did the GIAC Certified Forensic Analyst project team have the right skills?

457. Was it performed on time?

458. Will you need to provide essential services information about activities?

459. What is the activity inventory?

460. How do you fund change orders?

461. What are the audit requirements?

462. The impact and what actions were taken?

463. One way to define activities is to consider how organization employees describe jobs to families and friends. You basically want to know, What do you do?

464. Which contract type places the most risk on the seller?

465. Can you change your activities?

466. Why do you manage cost?

467. How do you allocate indirect costs to activities?

468. What defines a successful GIAC Certified Forensic Analyst project?

469. What is a GIAC Certified Forensic Analyst project Management Plan?

470. What is the activity recast of the budget?

471. Eac -estimate at completion, what is the total job expected to cost?

472. In which phase of the acquisition process cycle does source qualifications reside?

473. What were things that you did very well and want to do the same again on the next GIAC Certified Forensic Analyst project?

## 2.22 Cost Estimating Worksheet: GIAC Certified Forensic Analyst

474. What can be included?

475. What additional GIAC Certified Forensic Analyst project(s) could be initiated as a result of this GIAC Certified Forensic Analyst project?

476. Is the GIAC Certified Forensic Analyst project responsive to community need?

477. What costs are to be estimated?

478. What will others want?

479. Does the GIAC Certified Forensic Analyst project provide innovative ways for stakeholders to overcome obstacles or deliver better outcomes?

480. Identify the timeframe necessary to monitor progress and collect data to determine how the selected measure has changed?

481. Who is best positioned to know and assist in identifying corresponding factors?

482. Will the GIAC Certified Forensic Analyst project collaborate with the local community and leverage resources?

483. Ask: are others positioned to know, are others credible, and will others cooperate?

484. What happens to any remaining funds not used?

485. Is it feasible to establish a control group arrangement?

486. What is the estimated labor cost today based upon this information?

487. How will the results be shared and to whom?

488. What is the purpose of estimating?

489. Value pocket identification & quantification what are value pockets?

490. Can a trend be established from historical performance data on the selected measure and are the criteria for using trend analysis or forecasting methods met?

## 2.23 Cost Baseline: GIAC Certified Forensic Analyst

491. Does the suggested change request represent a desired enhancement to the products functionality?

492. Should a more thorough impact analysis be conducted?

493. How do you manage cost?

494. If you sold 10x widgets on a day, what would the affect on profits be?

495. How likely is it to go wrong?

496. What is your organizations history in doing similar tasks?

497. Have all approved changes to the schedule baseline been identified and impact on the GIAC Certified Forensic Analyst project documented?

498. Verify business objectives. Are others appropriate, and well-articulated?

499. Is there anything you need from upper management in order to be successful?

500. Have all the product or service deliverables been accepted by the customer?

501. When should cost estimates be developed?

502. Have all approved changes to the GIAC Certified Forensic Analyst project requirement been identified and impact on the performance, cost, and schedule baselines documented?

503. Vac -variance at completion, how much over/ under budget do you expect to be?

504. Review your risk triggers -have your risks changed?

505. How difficult will it be to do specific tasks on the GIAC Certified Forensic Analyst project?

506. What is the most important thing to do next to make your GIAC Certified Forensic Analyst project successful?

507. Has the GIAC Certified Forensic Analyst projected annual cost to operate and maintain the product(s) or service(s) been approved and funded?

508. Have the actual milestone completion dates been compared to the approved schedule?

509. How fast?

## 2.24 Quality Management Plan: GIAC Certified Forensic Analyst

510. How many GIAC Certified Forensic Analyst project staff does this specific process affect?

511. How do you decide what information to record?

512. Have all involved stakeholders and work groups committed to the GIAC Certified Forensic Analyst project?

513. How do you document and correct nonconformances?

514. No superfluous information or marketing narrative?

515. How are your organizations compensation and recognition approaches and the performance management system used to reinforce high performance?

516. How do you ensure that your sampling methods and procedures meet your data needs?

517. What would you gain if you spent time working to improve this process?

518. Does the GIAC Certified Forensic Analyst project have a formal GIAC Certified Forensic Analyst project Plan?

519. How do you decide what information needs to be recorded?

520. Is there a procedure for this process?

521. How do senior leaders create and communicate values and performance expectations?

522. How do senior leaders create your organizational focus on customers and other stakeholders?

523. Show/provide copy of procedures for taking field notes?

524. How will you know that a change is actually an improvement?

525. Account for the procedures used to verify the data quality of the data being reviewed?

526. How do you manage quality?

527. How is staff trained in procedures?

528. Contradictory information between document sections?

529. What is the return on investment?

## 2.25 Quality Metrics: GIAC Certified Forensic Analyst

530. How do you communicate results and findings to upper management?

531. What happens if you get an abnormal result?

532. How effective are your security tests?

533. Filter visualizations of interest?

534. Are applicable standards referenced and available?

535. Are documents on hand to provide explanations of privacy and confidentiality?

536. Subjective quality component: customer satisfaction, how do you measure it?

537. Is material complete (and does it meet the standards)?

538. How exactly do you define when differences exist?

539. Is the reporting frequency appropriate?

540. Do the operators focus on determining; is there anything you need to worry about?

541. Has it met internal or external standards?

542. When will the Final Guidance will be issued?

543. Who notifies stakeholders of normal and abnormal results?

544. The metrics–what is being considered?

545. Did the team meet the GIAC Certified Forensic Analyst project success criteria documented in the Quality Metrics Matrix?

546. Are quality metrics defined?

547. If the defect rate during testing is substantially higher than that of the previous release (or a similar product), then ask: Did you plan for and actually improve testing effectiveness?

548. What is the benchmark?

549. What are you trying to accomplish?

## 2.26 Process Improvement Plan: GIAC Certified Forensic Analyst

550. Does your process ensure quality?

551. Management commitment at all levels?

552. Modeling current processes is great, and will you ever see a return on that investment?

553. Have storage and access mechanisms and procedures been determined?

554. Have the supporting tools been developed or acquired?

555. What personnel are the coaches for your initiative?

556. Who should prepare the process improvement action plan?

557. Has a process guide to collect the data been developed?

558. If a process improvement framework is being used, which elements will help the problems and goals listed?

559. What makes people good SPI coaches?

560. Have the frequency of collection and the points in the process where measurements will be made

been determined?

561. The motive is determined by asking, Why do you want to achieve this goal?

562. What is quality and how will you ensure it?

563. Are you following the quality standards?

564. Are you making progress on the goals?

565. Does explicit definition of the measures exist?

566. What personnel are the champions for the initiative?

567. Are you making progress on the improvement framework?

568. What is the test-cycle concept?

## 2.27 Responsibility Assignment Matrix: GIAC Certified Forensic Analyst

569. Does the GIAC Certified Forensic Analyst project need to be analyzed further to uncover additional responsibilities?

570. GIAC Certified Forensic Analyst projected economic escalation?

571. Are the actual costs used for variance analysis reconcilable with data from the accounting system?

572. What is the primary purpose of the human resource plan?

573. Are estimates of costs at completion generated in a rational, consistent manner?

574. Who is going to do that work?

575. Evaluate the performance of operating organizations?

576. Is accountability placed at the lowest-possible level within the GIAC Certified Forensic Analyst project so that decisions can be made at that level?

577. Are your organizations and items of cost assigned to each pool identified?

578. Contract line items and end items?

579. Changes in the direct base to which overhead costs are allocated?

580. What are the assigned resources?

581. When performing is split among two or more roles, is the work clearly defined so that the efforts are coordinated and the communication is clear?

582. Authorization to proceed with all authorized work?

583. Will too many Communicating responsibilities tangle the GIAC Certified Forensic Analyst project in unnecessary communications?

584. Direct labor dollars and/or hours?

585. What will the work cost?

586. Too many is: do all the identified roles need to be routinely informed or only in exceptional circumstances?

587. With too many people labeled as doing the work, are there too many hands involved?

## 2.28 Roles and Responsibilities: GIAC Certified Forensic Analyst

588. Required skills, knowledge, experience?

589. Key conclusions and recommendations: Are conclusions and recommendations relevant and acceptable?

590. Where are you most strong as a supervisor?

591. To decide whether to use a quality measurement, ask how will you know when it is achieved?

592. Once the responsibilities are defined for the GIAC Certified Forensic Analyst project, have the deliverables, roles and responsibilities been clearly communicated to every participant?

593. Are GIAC Certified Forensic Analyst project team roles and responsibilities identified and documented?

594. Accountabilities: what are the roles and responsibilities of individual team members?

595. Who is responsible for implementation activities and where will the functions, roles and responsibilities be defined?

596. How is your work-life balance?

597. Implementation of actions: Who are the responsible units?

598. Are governance roles and responsibilities documented?

599. Do the values and practices inherent in the culture of your organization foster or hinder the process?

600. Was the expectation clearly communicated?

601. Is feedback clearly communicated and non-judgmental?

602. What is working well?

603. Are the quality assurance functions and related roles and responsibilities clearly defined?

604. Attainable / achievable: the goal is attainable; can you actually accomplish the goal?

605. Does your vision/mission support a culture of quality data?

606. Are GIAC Certified Forensic Analyst project team roles and responsibilities identified and documented?

607. Authority: what areas/GIAC Certified Forensic Analyst projects in your work do you have the authority to decide upon and act on the already stated decisions?

## 2.29 Human Resource Management Plan: GIAC Certified Forensic Analyst

608. Is an industry recognized support tool(s) being used for GIAC Certified Forensic Analyst project scheduling & tracking?

609. Has a provision been made to reassess GIAC Certified Forensic Analyst project risks at various GIAC Certified Forensic Analyst project stages?

610. Pareto diagrams, statistical sampling, flow charting or trend analysis used quality monitoring?

611. Is there a formal set of procedures supporting Issues Management?

612. Are milestone deliverables effectively tracked and compared to GIAC Certified Forensic Analyst project plan?

613. Were sponsors and decision makers available when needed outside regularly scheduled meetings?

614. Who is evaluated?

615. Have all unresolved risks been documented?

616. Is there a Quality Management Plan?

617. Are schedule deliverables actually delivered?

618. What commitments have been made?

619. Is there a formal set of procedures supporting Stakeholder Management?

620. Is there a formal process for updating the GIAC Certified Forensic Analyst project baseline?

621. Are trade-offs between accepting the risk and mitigating the risk identified?

622. Are vendor contract reports, reviews and visits conducted periodically?

623. Are key risk mitigation strategies added to the GIAC Certified Forensic Analyst project schedule?

## 2.30 Communications Management Plan: GIAC Certified Forensic Analyst

624. Who to learn from?

625. What to learn?

626. Who were proponents/opponents?

627. Who is involved as you identify stakeholders?

628. Why manage stakeholders?

629. Is there an important stakeholder who is actively opposed and will not receive messages?

630. Will messages be directly related to the release strategy or phases of the GIAC Certified Forensic Analyst project?

631. Do you then often overlook a key stakeholder or stakeholder group?

632. How did the term stakeholder originate?

633. Are there potential barriers between the team and the stakeholder?

634. How were corresponding initiatives successful?

635. What to know?

636. What is the stakeholders level of authority?

637. Are there too many who have an interest in some aspect of your work?

638. Are stakeholders internal or external?

639. Can you think of other people who might have concerns or interests?

640. Who did you turn to if you had questions?

641. Are the stakeholders getting the information others need, are others consulted, are concerns addressed?

642. Which team member will work with each stakeholder?

643. Why do you manage communications?

## 2.31 Risk Management Plan: GIAC Certified Forensic Analyst

644. Is the technology to be built new to your organization?

645. Are the required plans included, such as nonstructural flood risk management plans?

646. Which is an input to the risk management process?

647. Which risks should get the attention?

648. Methodology: how will risk management be performed on this GIAC Certified Forensic Analyst project?

649. What does a risk management program do?

650. Why is product liability a serious issue?

651. Havent software GIAC Certified Forensic Analyst projects been late before?

652. How is risk response planning performed?

653. Market risk -will the new service or product be useful to your organization or marketable to others?

654. Has something like this been done before?

655. Mitigation -how can you avoid the risk?

656. Costs associated with late delivery or a defective product?

657. Where are you confronted with risks during the business phases?

658. Are flexibility and reuse paramount?

659. Can you stabilize dynamic risk factors?

660. Is GIAC Certified Forensic Analyst project scope stable?

661. Can the GIAC Certified Forensic Analyst project proceed without assuming the risk?

662. Minimize cost and financial risk?

663. Maximize short-term return on investment?

## 2.32 Risk Register: GIAC Certified Forensic Analyst

664. Risk probability and impact: how will the probabilities and impacts of risk items be assessed?

665. Schedule impact/severity estimated range (workdays) assume the event happens, what is the potential impact?

666. Technology risk -is the GIAC Certified Forensic Analyst project technically feasible?

667. Are there other alternative controls that could be implemented?

668. Assume the risk event or situation happens, what would the impact be?

669. Are your objectives at risk?

670. Having taken action, how did the responses effect change, and where is the GIAC Certified Forensic Analyst project now?

671. When will it happen?

672. What are the assumptions and current status that support the assessment of the risk?

673. What are you going to do to limit the GIAC Certified Forensic Analyst projects risk exposure due to the identified risks?

674. What will be done?

675. What could prevent you delivering on the strategic program objectives and what is being done to mitigate corresponding issues?

676. What is your current and future risk profile?

677. What are the main aims, objectives of the policy, strategy, or service and the intended outcomes?

678. How well are risks controlled?

679. What has changed since the last period?

680. How are risks graded?

681. Who is going to do it?

682. Have other controls and solutions been implemented in other services which could be applied as an alternative to additional funding?

## 2.33 Probability and Impact Assessment: GIAC Certified Forensic Analyst

683. Do you train all developers in the process?

684. Are formal technical reviews part of this process?

685. What is the experience (performance, attitude, business ethics, etc.) in the past with contractors?

686. How solid is the GIAC Certified Forensic Analyst projection of competitive reaction?

687. Who are the international/overseas GIAC Certified Forensic Analyst project partners (equipment supplier/supplier/consultant/contractor) for this GIAC Certified Forensic Analyst project?

688. Is a software GIAC Certified Forensic Analyst project management tool available?

689. Do end-users have realistic expectations?

690. Does the GIAC Certified Forensic Analyst project team have experience with the technology to be implemented?

691. Do the requirements require the creation of new algorithms?

692. What things are likely to change?

693. Risks should be identified during which phase of GIAC Certified Forensic Analyst project management life cycle?

694. When and how will the recent breakthroughs in basic research lead to commercial products?

695. Are some people working on multiple GIAC Certified Forensic Analyst projects?

696. Will there be an increase in the political conservatism?

697. Are testing tools available and suitable?

698. Anticipated volatility of the requirements?

699. Do you have a mechanism for managing change?

700. What should be done with non-critical risks?

## 2.34 Probability and Impact Matrix: GIAC Certified Forensic Analyst

701. Which should be probably done NEXT?

702. Are the risk data timely and relevant?

703. Do you manage the process through use of metrics?

704. Have staff received necessary training?

705. Do the people have the right combinations of skills?

706. Do requirements put excessive performance constraints on the product?

707. Risk may be made during which step of risk management?

708. Could others have been better mitigated?

709. My GIAC Certified Forensic Analyst project leader has suddenly left your organization, what do you do?

710. Are staff committed for the duration of the GIAC Certified Forensic Analyst project?

711. During GIAC Certified Forensic Analyst project executing, a major problem occurs that was not included in the risk register. What should you do FIRST?

712. Are tool mentors available?

713. How are the local factors going to affect the absorption?

714. What would be the effect of slippage?

715. Is security a central objective?

716. Have customers been involved fully in the definition of requirements?

717. What did not work so well?

718. Are the best people available?

719. What will be the impact or consequence if the risk occurs?

## 2.35 Risk Data Sheet: GIAC Certified Forensic Analyst

720. What if client refuses?

721. What can happen?

722. What do you know?

723. If it happens, what are the consequences?

724. Has a sensitivity analysis been carried out?

725. What do people affected think about the need for, and practicality of preventive measures?

726. What are you trying to achieve (Objectives)?

727. What are you weak at and therefore need to do better?

728. Whom do you serve (customers)?

729. During work activities could hazards exist?

730. How can hazards be reduced?

731. What is the environment within which you operate (social trends, economic, community values, broad based participation, national directions etc.)?

732. What can you do?

733. What is the likelihood of it happening?

734. Are new hazards created?

735. How reliable is the data source?

736. Risk of what?

737. What is the duration of infection (the length of time the host is infected with the organizm) in a normal healthy human host?

738. What was measured?

739. Will revised controls lead to tolerable risk levels?

# 2.36 Procurement Management Plan: GIAC Certified Forensic Analyst

740. Are the payment terms being followed?

741. What areas are overlooked on this GIAC Certified Forensic Analyst project?

742. Have reserves been created to address risks?

743. Do you have the reasons why the changes to your organizational systems and capabilities are required?

744. Are risk triggers captured?

745. Is pert / critical path or equivalent methodology being used?

746. Are GIAC Certified Forensic Analyst project leaders committed to this GIAC Certified Forensic Analyst project full time?

747. GIAC Certified Forensic Analyst project Objectives?

748. Is stakeholder involvement adequate?

749. Are cause and effect determined for risks when others occur?

750. Are GIAC Certified Forensic Analyst project team members committed fulltime?

751. Are GIAC Certified Forensic Analyst project team roles and responsibilities identified and documented?

752. Have the key elements of a coherent GIAC Certified Forensic Analyst project management strategy been established?

753. Has GIAC Certified Forensic Analyst project success criteria been defined?

754. How will the duration of the GIAC Certified Forensic Analyst project influence your decisions?

## 2.37 Source Selection Criteria: GIAC Certified Forensic Analyst

755. If the costs are normalized, please account for how the normalization is conducted. Is a cost realism analysis used?

756. Are evaluators ready to begin this task?

757. When is it appropriate to conduct a preproposal conference?

758. What source selection software is your team using?

759. Are there any specific considerations that precludes offers from being selected as the awardee?

760. When should debriefings be held and how should they be scheduled?

761. Can you make a cost/technical tradeoff?

762. Does an evaluation need to include the identification of strengths and weaknesses?

763. Have team members been adequately trained?

764. What should a Draft Request for Proposal (DRFP) include?

765. Are they compliant with all technical requirements?

766. How should the preproposal conference be conducted?

767. What past performance information should be requested?

768. Has all proposal data been loaded?

769. Are there any common areas of weaknesses or deficiencies in the proposals in the competitive range?

770. Are types/quantities of material, facilities appropriate?

771. Do you prepare an independent cost estimate?

772. How should the oral presentations be handled?

773. What risks were identified in the proposals?

774. Who is on the Source Selection Advisory Committee?

## 2.38 Stakeholder Management Plan: GIAC Certified Forensic Analyst

775. What are reporting requirements?

776. What are the criteria for selecting suppliers of off the shelf products?

777. Who would sign off on the charter?

778. Has a sponsor been identified?

779. Where to get additional help?

780. Does a documented GIAC Certified Forensic Analyst project organizational policy & plan (i.e. governance model) exist?

781. What potential impact does the GIAC Certified Forensic Analyst project have on the stakeholder?

782. Are corrective actions and variances reported?

783. Have key stakeholders been identified?

784. Are requirements management tracking tools and procedures in place?

785. Have stakeholder accountabilities & responsibilities been clearly defined?

786. What guidelines or procedures currently exist that must be adhered to (eg departmental accounting

procedures)?

787. How many GIAC Certified Forensic Analyst project staff does this specific process affect?

788. Does the GIAC Certified Forensic Analyst project have a formal GIAC Certified Forensic Analyst project Charter?

789. Will all outputs delivered by the GIAC Certified Forensic Analyst project follow the same process?

790. Are the schedule estimates reasonable given the GIAC Certified Forensic Analyst project?

791. Why is it important to reduce deliverables to a smallest component?

# 2.39 Change Management Plan: GIAC Certified Forensic Analyst

792. What are the specific target groups/audiences that will be impacted by this change?

793. How many people are required in each of the roles?

794. Have the business unit contacts been selected and notified?

795. Change invariability confront many relationships especially the already stated that require a set of behaviours What roles with in your organization are affected and how?

796. Will a different work structure focus people on what is important?

797. What are you trying to achieve as a result of communication?

798. What new competencies will be required for the roles?

799. Readiness -what is a successful end state?

800. What is the worst thing that can happen if you chose not to communicate this information?

801. What type of materials/channels will be available to leverage?

802. Is there a support model for this application and are the details available for distribution?

803. What are the essentials of the message?

804. Has the training co-ordinator been provided with the training details and put in place the necessary arrangements?

805. Are there resource implications for your communications strategy?

806. How will you deal with anger about the restricting of communications due to confidentiality considerations?

807. What is the reason for the communication?

808. Where do you want to be?

809. What do you expect the target audience to do, say, think or feel as a result of this communication?

810. Have the business unit contacts been briefed by the GIAC Certified Forensic Analyst project team?

811. Is it the same for each of the business units?

# 3.0 Executing Process Group: GIAC Certified Forensic Analyst

812. What type of information goes in the quality assurance plan?

813. What areas does the group agree are the biggest success on the GIAC Certified Forensic Analyst project?

814. Will additional funds be needed for hardware or software?

815. What good practices or successful experiences or transferable examples have been identified?

816. What are the typical GIAC Certified Forensic Analyst project management skills?

817. What are some crucial elements of a good GIAC Certified Forensic Analyst project plan?

818. How well defined and documented were the GIAC Certified Forensic Analyst project management processes you chose to use?

819. Could a new application negatively affect the current IT infrastructure?

820. Specific - is the objective clear in terms of what, how, when, and where the situation will be changed?

821. What areas were overlooked on this GIAC

Certified Forensic Analyst project?

822. What is the difference between using brainstorming and the Delphi technique for risk identification?

823. Are the necessary foundations in place to ensure the sustainability of the results of the programme?

824. How well did the team follow the chosen processes?

825. How can you use Microsoft GIAC Certified Forensic Analyst project and Excel to assist in GIAC Certified Forensic Analyst project risk management?

826. In what way has the program come up with innovative measures for problem-solving?

827. Is activity definition the first process involved in GIAC Certified Forensic Analyst project time management?

828. Is the GIAC Certified Forensic Analyst project making progress in helping to achieve the set results?

# 3.1 Team Member Status Report: GIAC Certified Forensic Analyst

829. Is there evidence that staff is taking a more professional approach toward management of your organizations GIAC Certified Forensic Analyst projects?

830. Does every department have to have a GIAC Certified Forensic Analyst project Manager on staff?

831. What is to be done?

832. Are the products of your organizations GIAC Certified Forensic Analyst projects meeting customers objectives?

833. How it is to be done?

834. When a teams productivity and success depend on collaboration and the efficient flow of information, what generally fails them?

835. Are the attitudes of staff regarding GIAC Certified Forensic Analyst project work improving?

836. How much risk is involved?

837. Does the product, good, or service already exist within your organization?

838. The problem with Reward & Recognition Programs is that the truly deserving people all too

often get left out. How can you make it practical?

839. Will the staff do training or is that done by a third party?

840. How will resource planning be done?

841. What specific interest groups do you have in place?

842. Why is it to be done?

843. Do you have an Enterprise GIAC Certified Forensic Analyst project Management Office (EPMO)?

844. Does your organization have the means (staff, money, contract, etc.) to produce or to acquire the product, good, or service?

845. How does this product, good, or service meet the needs of the GIAC Certified Forensic Analyst project and your organization as a whole?

846. Are your organizations GIAC Certified Forensic Analyst projects more successful over time?

847. How can you make it practical?

## 3.2 Change Request: GIAC Certified Forensic Analyst

848. How does your organization control changes before and after software is released to a customer?

849. How are changes requested (forms, method of communication)?

850. Are change requests logged and managed?

851. What type of changes does change control take into account?

852. How do team members communicate with each other?

853. Who needs to approve change requests?

854. Has your address changed?

855. Who is communicating the change?

856. What is a Change Request Form?

857. What has an inspector to inspect and to check?

858. Who can suggest changes?

859. Have all related configuration items been properly updated?

860. How is the change documented (format, content,

storage)?

861. What are the Impacts to your organization?

862. Does the schedule include GIAC Certified Forensic Analyst project management time and change request analysis time?

863. Change request coordination ?

864. How to get changes (code) out in a timely manner?

865. What is the purpose of change control?

866. Is it feasible to use requirements attributes as predictors of reliability?

867. Since there are no change requests in your GIAC Certified Forensic Analyst project at this point, what must you have before you begin?

# 3.3 Change Log: GIAC Certified Forensic Analyst

868. Is the change request open, closed or pending?

869. Is the requested change request a result of changes in other GIAC Certified Forensic Analyst project(s)?

870. When was the request submitted?

871. Do the described changes impact on the integrity or security of the system?

872. Who initiated the change request?

873. Does the suggested change request seem to represent a necessary enhancement to the product?

874. Where do changes come from?

875. Is the submitted change a new change or a modification of a previously approved change?

876. Will the GIAC Certified Forensic Analyst project fail if the change request is not executed?

877. Is the change backward compatible without limitations?

878. Is this a mandatory replacement?

879. How does this change affect scope?

880. When was the request approved?

881. How does this change affect the timeline of the schedule?

882. How does this relate to the standards developed for specific business processes?

883. Is the change request within GIAC Certified Forensic Analyst project scope?

# 3.4 Decision Log: GIAC Certified Forensic Analyst

884. Is your opponent open to a non-traditional workflow, or will it likely challenge anything you do?

885. Is everything working as expected?

886. Behaviors; what are guidelines that the team has identified that will assist them with getting the most out of team meetings?

887. With whom was the decision shared or considered?

888. How do you define success?

889. Does anything need to be adjusted?

890. What is the line where eDiscovery ends and document review begins?

891. What is your overall strategy for quality control / quality assurance procedures?

892. Linked to original objective?

893. Who will be given a copy of this document and where will it be kept?

894. What alternatives/risks were considered?

895. What are the cost implications?

896. Who is the decisionmaker?

897. Meeting purpose; why does this team meet?

898. Which variables make a critical difference?

899. At what point in time does loss become unacceptable?

900. How effective is maintaining the log at facilitating organizational learning?

901. How does an increasing emphasis on cost containment influence the strategies and tactics used?

902. How does provision of information, both in terms of content and presentation, influence acceptance of alternative strategies?

903. What makes you different or better than others companies selling the same thing?

# 3.5 Quality Audit: GIAC Certified Forensic Analyst

904. Are all complaints involving the possible failure of a device, labeling, or packaging to meet any of its specifications reviewed, evaluated, and investigated?

905. How does your organization know that it is maintaining a conducive staff climate?

906. How does your organization know that its teaching activities (and staff learning) are effectively and constructively enhanced by its activities?

907. How does your organization know that its systems for providing high quality consultancy services to external parties are appropriately effective and constructive?

908. Quality is about improvement and accountability. The immediate questions that arise out of that statement are: (i) improvement on what, and (ii) accountable to whom?

909. How does your organization know that its quality of teaching is appropriately effective and constructive?

910. Has a written procedure been established to identify devices during all stages of receipt, reconditioning, distribution and installation so that mix-ups are prevented?

911. How does your organization know that its management system is appropriately effective and constructive?

912. How does your organization know that the system for managing its facilities is appropriately effective and constructive?

913. How does your organization know that its Governance system is appropriately effective and constructive?

914. Do the acceptance procedures and specifications include the criteria for acceptance/rejection, define the process to be used, and specify the measuring and test equipment that is to be used?

915. Are all employees including salespersons made aware that they must report all complaints received from any source for inclusion in the complaint handling system?

916. How does your organization know that its staff financial services are appropriately effective and constructive?

917. Are complaint files maintained?

918. How does your organization know that it is appropriately effective and constructive in preparing its staff for organizational aspirations?

919. How does your organization know that its systems for assisting staff with career planning and employment placements are appropriately effective and constructive?

920. How does your organization know that its promotions system is appropriately effective, constructive and fair?

921. Are all records associated with the reconditioning of a device maintained for a minimum of two years after the sale or disposal of the last device within a lot of merchandise?

922. How does your organization know that its system for recruiting the best staff possible are appropriately effective and constructive?

923. Is there a written procedure for receiving materials?

## 3.6 Team Directory: GIAC Certified Forensic Analyst

924. Does a GIAC Certified Forensic Analyst project team directory list all resources assigned to the GIAC Certified Forensic Analyst project?

925. Days from the time the issue is identified?

926. How do unidentified risks impact the outcome of the GIAC Certified Forensic Analyst project?

927. Who are the Team Members?

928. Process decisions: which organizational elements and which individuals will be assigned management functions?

929. Where will the product be used and/or delivered or built when appropriate?

930. Process decisions: do job conditions warrant additional actions to collect job information and document on-site activity?

931. How and in what format should information be presented?

932. Do purchase specifications and configurations match requirements?

933. How does the team resolve conflicts and ensure tasks are completed?

934. Process decisions: are all start-up, turn over and close out requirements of the contract satisfied?

935. Who are your stakeholders (customers, sponsors, end users, team members)?

936. Who should receive information (all stakeholders)?

937. How will the team handle changes?

938. Decisions: is the most suitable form of contract being used?

939. Why is the work necessary?

940. What are you going to deliver or accomplish?

941. Is construction on schedule?

## 3.7 Team Operating Agreement: GIAC Certified Forensic Analyst

942. Are team roles clearly defined and accepted?

943. Did you delegate tasks such as taking meeting minutes, presenting a topic and soliciting input?

944. Does your team need access to all documents and information at all times?

945. Do you vary your voice pace, tone and pitch to engage participants and gain involvement?

946. What are the boundaries (organizational or geographic) within which you operate?

947. Have you set the goals and objectives of the team?

948. Do you prevent individuals from dominating the meeting?

949. What is the anticipated procedure (recruitment, solicitation of volunteers, or assignment) for selecting team members?

950. Do you post meeting notes and the recording (if used) and notify participants?

951. Do you brief absent members after they view meeting notes or listen to a recording?

952. Did you recap the meeting purpose, time, and expectations?

953. Do you send out the agenda and meeting materials in advance?

954. Do you begin with a question to engage everyone?

955. How will you resolve conflict efficiently and respectfully?

956. Have you established procedures that team members can follow to work effectively together, such as a team operating agreement?

957. Do you solicit member feedback about meetings and what would make them better?

958. Conflict resolution: how will disputes and other conflicts be mediated or resolved?

959. What administrative supports will be put in place to support the team and the teams supervisor?

960. Are leadership responsibilities shared among team members (versus a single leader)?

961. Reimbursements: how will the team members be reimbursed for expenses and time commitments?

# 3.8 Team Performance Assessment: GIAC Certified Forensic Analyst

962. To what degree is the team cognizant of small wins to be celebrated along the way?

963. To what degree will the team ensure that all members equitably share the work essential to the success of the team?

964. How much interpersonal friction is there in your team?

965. To what degree can team members meet frequently enough to accomplish the teams ends?

966. To what degree are the relative importance and priority of the goals clear to all team members?

967. To what degree do members articulate the goals beyond the team membership?

968. Do you promptly inform members about major developments that may affect them?

969. How do you keep key people outside the group informed about its accomplishments?

970. To what degree does the teams work approach provide opportunity for members to engage in results-based evaluation?

971. Individual task proficiency and team process

behavior: what is important for team functioning?

972. What do you think is the most constructive thing that could be done now to resolve considerations and disputes about method variance?

973. How hard do you try to make a good selection?

974. What structural changes have you made or are you preparing to make?

975. To what degree are the goals ambitious?

976. To what degree will the team adopt a concrete, clearly understood, and agreed-upon approach that will result in achievement of the teams goals?

977. To what degree does the teams purpose constitute a broader, deeper aspiration than just accomplishing short-term goals?

978. To what degree will new and supplemental skills be introduced as the need is recognized?

979. To what degree does the teams approach to its work allow for modification and improvement over time?

980. To what degree can the team measure progress against specific goals?

981. Lack of method variance in self-reported affect and perceptions at work: Reality or artifact?

# 3.9 Team Member Performance Assessment: GIAC Certified Forensic Analyst

982. What are the basic principles and objectives of performance measurement and assessment?

983. To what extent are systems and applications (e.g., game engine, mobile device platform) utilized?

984. Which training platform formats (i.e., mobile, virtual, videogame-based) were implemented in your effort(s)?

985. To what degree do team members understand one anothers roles and skills?

986. How is the timing of assessments organized (e.g., pre/post-test, single point during training, multiple reassessment during training)?

987. How is your organizations Strategic Management System tied to performance measurement?

988. To what degree do team members frequently explore the teams purpose and its implications?

989. To what degree are the goals realistic?

990. For what period of time is a member rated?

991. What are best practices for delivering and developing training evaluations to maximize the

benefits of leveraging emerging technologies?

992. Does adaptive training work?

993. How do you implement Cost Reduction?

994. To what degree do team members articulate the teams work approach?

995. What are the evaluation strategies (e.g., reaction, learning, behavior, results) used. What evaluation results did you have?

996. What variables that affect team members achievement are within your control?

997. In what areas would you like to concentrate your knowledge and resources?

998. How often are assessments to be conducted?

999. What are the key duties or tasks of the Ratee?

# 3.10 Issue Log: GIAC Certified Forensic Analyst

1000. What is the impact on the risks?

1001. What are the stakeholders interrelationships?

1002. Is access to the Issue Log controlled?

1003. How often do you engage with stakeholders?

1004. How do you manage communications?

1005. What help do you and your team need from the stakeholders?

1006. Do you feel a register helps?

1007. What is the impact on the Business Case?

1008. What steps can you take for positive relationships?

1009. Which stakeholders are thought leaders, influences, or early adopters?

1010. In classifying stakeholders, which approach to do so are you using?

1011. Can an impact cause deviation beyond team, stage or GIAC Certified Forensic Analyst project tolerances?

1012. Are the GIAC Certified Forensic Analyst project issues uniquely identified, including to which product they refer?

1013. What is the stakeholders political influence?

1014. In your work, how much time is spent on stakeholder identification?

# 4.0 Monitoring and Controlling Process Group: GIAC Certified Forensic Analyst

1015. Who needs to be engaged upfront to ensure use of results?

1016. What resources are necessary?

1017. How many more potential communications channels were introduced by the discovery of the new stakeholders?

1018. How is agile portfolio management done?

1019. What areas were overlooked on this GIAC Certified Forensic Analyst project?

1020. Does the solution fit in with organizations technical architectural requirements?

1021. Just how important is your work to the overall success of the GIAC Certified Forensic Analyst project?

1022. Based on your GIAC Certified Forensic Analyst project communication management plan, what worked well?

1023. Were escalated issues resolved promptly?

1024. What were things that you did very well and want to do the same again on the next GIAC Certified Forensic Analyst project?

1025. Is progress on outcomes due to your program?

1026. How well defined and documented were the GIAC Certified Forensic Analyst project management processes you chose to use?

1027. What departments are involved in its daily operation?

1028. How are you doing?

1029. Use: how will they use the information?

1030. Who are the GIAC Certified Forensic Analyst project stakeholders?

1031. How well did you do?

# 4.1 Project Performance Report: GIAC Certified Forensic Analyst

1032. To what degree does the teams work approach provide opportunity for members to engage in open interaction?

1033. To what degree can team members frequently and easily communicate with one another?

1034. What is in it for you?

1035. To what degree are the skill areas critical to team performance present?

1036. To what degree are the structures of the formal organization consistent with the behaviors in the informal organization?

1037. What is the degree to which rules govern information exchange between individuals within your organization?

1038. To what degree do the goals specify concrete team work products?

1039. To what degree are fresh input and perspectives systematically caught and added (for example, through information and analysis, new members, and senior sponsors)?

1040. To what degree is there a sense that only the team can succeed?

1041. To what degree does the informal organization make use of individual resources and meet individual needs?

1042. To what degree do individual skills and abilities match task demands?

1043. Next Steps?

1044. To what degree will the approach capitalize on and enhance the skills of all team members in a manner that takes into consideration other demands on members of the team?

1045. To what degree do all members feel responsible for all agreed-upon measures?

1046. What is the degree to which rules govern information exchange between groups?

1047. To what degree do team members feel that the purpose of the team is important, if not exciting?

# 4.2 Variance Analysis: GIAC Certified Forensic Analyst

1048. Are there quarterly budgets with quarterly performance comparisons?

1049. How do you manage changes in the nature of the overhead requirements?

1050. What is the performance to date and material commitment?

1051. Why are standard cost systems used?

1052. Wbs elements contractually specified for reporting of status to your organization (lowest level only)?

1053. What causes selling price variance?

1054. At what point should variances be isolated and brought to the attention of the management?

1055. What is the budgeted cost for work scheduled?

1056. What business event causes fluctuations?

1057. What is the total budget for the GIAC Certified Forensic Analyst project (including estimates for authorized and unpriced work)?

1058. Are the overhead pools formally and adequately identified?

1059. Did an existing competitor change strategy?

1060. Is budgeted cost for work performed calculated in a manner consistent with the way work is planned?

1061. How does your organization allocate the cost of shared expenses and services?

1062. Are all authorized tasks assigned to identified organizational elements?

1063. Budgeted cost for work performed?

1064. What should management do?

1065. Historical experience?

1066. Why do variances exist?

1067. Did your organization lose existing customers and/or gain new customers?

# 4.3 Earned Value Status: GIAC Certified Forensic Analyst

1068. Verification is a process of ensuring that the developed system satisfies the stakeholders agreements and specifications; Are you building the product right? What do you haverify?

1069. When is it going to finish?

1070. Validation is a process of ensuring that the developed system will actually achieve the stakeholders desired outcomes; Are you building the right product? What do you validate?

1071. How much is it going to cost by the finish?

1072. Are you hitting your GIAC Certified Forensic Analyst projects targets?

1073. Earned value can be used in almost any GIAC Certified Forensic Analyst project situation and in almost any GIAC Certified Forensic Analyst project environment. it may be used on large GIAC Certified Forensic Analyst projects, medium sized GIAC Certified Forensic Analyst projects, tiny GIAC Certified Forensic Analyst projects (in cut-down form), complex and simple GIAC Certified Forensic Analyst projects and in any market sector. some people, of course, know all about earned value, they have used it for years - but perhaps not as effectively as they could have?

1074. If earned value management (EVM) is so good in determining the true status of a GIAC Certified Forensic Analyst project and GIAC Certified Forensic Analyst project its completion, why is it that hardly any one uses it in information systems related GIAC Certified Forensic Analyst projects?

1075. Where are your problem areas?

1076. How does this compare with other GIAC Certified Forensic Analyst projects?

1077. Where is evidence-based earned value in your organization reported?

1078. What is the unit of forecast value?

# 4.4 Risk Audit: GIAC Certified Forensic Analyst

1079. Have you reviewed your constitution within the last twelve months?

1080. Does your organization have a register of insurance policies detailing all current insurance policies?

1081. Have all involved been advised of any obligations they have to sponsors?

1082. What impact does prior experience have on decisions made during the risk-assessment process?

1083. Who audits the auditor?

1084. Do you meet all obligations relating to funds secured from grants, loans and sponsors?

1085. How do you compare to other jurisdictions when managing the risk of ....?

1086. Are some people working on multiple GIAC Certified Forensic Analyst projects?

1087. Do you have an understanding of insurance claims processes?

1088. How risk averse are you?

1089. How effective are your risk controls?

1090. Risks with GIAC Certified Forensic Analyst projects or new initiatives?

1091. What are the Internal Controls ?

1092. How do you manage risk?

1093. Is there (or should there be) some impact on the process of setting materiality when the auditor more effectively identifies higher risk areas of the financial statements?

1094. Do all coaches/instructors/leaders have appropriate and current accreditation?

1095. Are the software tools integrated with each other?

1096. Is a software GIAC Certified Forensic Analyst project management tool available?

1097. Strategic business risk audit methodologies; are corresponding an attempt to sell other services, and is management becoming the client of the audit rather than the shareholder?

# 4.5 Contractor Status Report: GIAC Certified Forensic Analyst

1098. What was the budget or estimated cost for your organizations services?

1099. Are there contractual transfer concerns?

1100. Describe how often regular updates are made to the proposed solution. Are corresponding regular updates included in the standard maintenance plan?

1101. What was the final actual cost?

1102. What are the minimum and optimal bandwidth requirements for the proposed soluiton?

1103. What process manages the contracts?

1104. How long have you been using the services?

1105. Who can list a GIAC Certified Forensic Analyst project as organization experience, your organization or a previous employee of your organization?

1106. How is risk transferred?

1107. What was the overall budget or estimated cost?

1108. What was the actual budget or estimated cost for your organizations services?

1109. If applicable; describe your standard schedule

for new software version releases. Are new software version releases included in the standard maintenance plan?

1110. What is the average response time for answering a support call?

# 4.6 Formal Acceptance: GIAC Certified Forensic Analyst

1111. Who supplies data?

1112. Was the GIAC Certified Forensic Analyst project goal achieved?

1113. General estimate of the costs and times to complete the GIAC Certified Forensic Analyst project?

1114. How does your team plan to obtain formal acceptance on your GIAC Certified Forensic Analyst project?

1115. Was the GIAC Certified Forensic Analyst project managed well?

1116. What was done right?

1117. Do you perform formal acceptance or burn-in tests?

1118. Did the GIAC Certified Forensic Analyst project manager and team act in a professional and ethical manner?

1119. What lessons were learned about your GIAC Certified Forensic Analyst project management methodology?

1120. Was business value realized?

1121. How well did the team follow the methodology?

1122. Was the client satisfied with the GIAC Certified Forensic Analyst project results?

1123. Does it do what GIAC Certified Forensic Analyst project team said it would?

1124. Who would use it?

1125. What is the Acceptance Management Process?

1126. Did the GIAC Certified Forensic Analyst project achieve its MOV?

1127. Was the sponsor/customer satisfied?

1128. Do you buy-in installation services?

1129. What function(s) does it fill or meet?

1130. Do you buy pre-configured systems or build your own configuration?

# 5.0 Closing Process Group: GIAC Certified Forensic Analyst

1131. What could have been improved?

1132. What will you do?

1133. What areas were overlooked on this GIAC Certified Forensic Analyst project?

1134. How will staff learn how to use the deliverables?

1135. If a risk event occurs, what will you do?

1136. Will the GIAC Certified Forensic Analyst project deliverable(s) replace a current asset or group of assets?

1137. What were things that you did well, and could improve, and how?

1138. What business situation is being addressed?

1139. How critical is the GIAC Certified Forensic Analyst project success to the success of your organization?

1140. What areas does the group agree are the biggest success on the GIAC Certified Forensic Analyst project?

1141. How will you do it?

1142. What is the risk of failure to your organization?

1143. What is the GIAC Certified Forensic Analyst project name and date of completion?

1144. Who are the GIAC Certified Forensic Analyst project stakeholders?

1145. Were decisions made in a timely manner?

1146. Were cost budgets met?

1147. Based on your GIAC Certified Forensic Analyst project communication management plan, what worked well?

# 5.1 Procurement Audit: GIAC Certified Forensic Analyst

1148. Are there mechanisms for evaluating the departments suppliers performance in relation to prices, quality, delivery and innovation?

1149. Are eu procurement regulations applicable?

1150. Are the supporting documents for payments voided or cancelled following payment?

1151. Did your organization calculate the contract value accurately?

1152. Were technical requirements set strict enough to guarantee the desired performance without being unnecessarily tight to exclude favourable bids that do not comply with all requirements?

1153. Is it calculated whether aggregated procurement can be more cost-efficient?

1154. Are all checks stored in a secure area?

1155. Where funding is being arranged by borrowings, do corresponding have the necessary approval and legal authority?

1156. Is there a procedure to summarize bids and select a vendor?

1157. Was confidentiality ensured when necessary?

1158. Is the issuance of purchase orders scheduled so that orders are not issued daily?

1159. Was the expert likely to gain privileged knowledge from his activity which could be advantageous for him in a subsequent competition?

1160. Are sub-criteria clearly indicated?

1161. Was the chosen procedure the most efficient and effective for the performance of the contract?

1162. Has your organization procedures in place to monitor the input of experts employed to assist the procurement function?

1163. How are you making the audit trail easy to follow?

1164. Who had not previously applied to participate?

1165. Are procedures established on how orders will be shipped?

1166. Are prices always included on the purchase order?

1167. In open and restricted procedures, did the contracting authority make sure that there is no substantive change to the bid due to this clearing process?

## 5.2 Contract Close-Out: GIAC Certified Forensic Analyst

1168. Have all contracts been completed?

1169. Have all contract records been included in the GIAC Certified Forensic Analyst project archives?

1170. Parties: Authorized?

1171. Change in knowledge?

1172. Parties: who is involved?

1173. How does it work?

1174. Has each contract been audited to verify acceptance and delivery?

1175. Why Outsource?

1176. What happens to the recipient of services?

1177. Change in attitude or behavior?

1178. How/when used ?

1179. Are the signers the authorized officials?

1180. Change in circumstances?

1181. What is capture management?

1182. Was the contract type appropriate?

1183. Have all contracts been closed?

1184. How is the contracting office notified of the automatic contract close-out?

1185. Have all acceptance criteria been met prior to final payment to contractors?

1186. Was the contract complete without requiring numerous changes and revisions?

1187. Was the contract sufficiently clear so as not to result in numerous disputes and misunderstandings?

## 5.3 Project or Phase Close-Out: GIAC Certified Forensic Analyst

1188. What information is each stakeholder group interested in?

1189. What security considerations needed to be addressed during the procurement life cycle?

1190. Did the GIAC Certified Forensic Analyst project management methodology work?

1191. What can you do better next time, and what specific actions can you take to improve?

1192. What were the goals and objectives of the communications strategy for the GIAC Certified Forensic Analyst project?

1193. Who exerted influence that has positively affected or negatively impacted the GIAC Certified Forensic Analyst project?

1194. Was the schedule met?

1195. What were the desired outcomes?

1196. Does the lesson describe a function that would be done differently the next time?

1197. What was learned?

1198. How often did each stakeholder need an

update?

1199. Which changes might a stakeholder be required to make as a result of the GIAC Certified Forensic Analyst project?

1200. Were risks identified and mitigated?

1201. Can the lesson learned be replicated?

1202. Complete yes or no?

1203. What are they?

1204. In preparing the Lessons Learned report, should it reflect a consensus viewpoint, or should the report reflect the different individual viewpoints?

1205. What is a Risk Management Process?

1206. What are the mandatory communication needs for each stakeholder?

# 5.4 Lessons Learned: GIAC Certified Forensic Analyst

1207. How effective were Best Practices & Lessons Learned from prior GIAC Certified Forensic Analyst projects utilized in this GIAC Certified Forensic Analyst project?

1208. Is there a clear cause and effect between the activity and the lesson learned?

1209. What was the methodology behind successful learning experiences, and how might they be applied to the broader challenge of your organizations knowledge management?

1210. How was the political and social history changed over the life of the GIAC Certified Forensic Analyst project?

1211. How well defined were the acceptance criteria for GIAC Certified Forensic Analyst project deliverables?

1212. How well prepared were you to receive GIAC Certified Forensic Analyst project deliverables?

1213. Was the user/client satisfied with the end product?

1214. Whom to share Lessons Learned Information with?

1215. How well did the GIAC Certified Forensic Analyst project Manager respond to questions or comments related to the GIAC Certified Forensic Analyst project?

1216. How useful and complete was the GIAC Certified Forensic Analyst project document repository?

1217. How objective was the collection of data?

1218. How well were expectations met regarding the frequency and content of information that was conveyed to by the GIAC Certified Forensic Analyst project Manager?

1219. What things mattered the most on this GIAC Certified Forensic Analyst project?

1220. What regulatory regime controlled how your organization head and program manager directed your organization and GIAC Certified Forensic Analyst project?

1221. Were the GIAC Certified Forensic Analyst project goals attained?

1222. For the next GIAC Certified Forensic Analyst project, how could you improve on the way GIAC Certified Forensic Analyst project was conducted?

1223. What was the geopolitical history during the origin of your organization and at the time of task input?

1224. What worked well or did not work well, either for this GIAC Certified Forensic Analyst project or for the GIAC Certified Forensic Analyst project team?

1225. To what extent was the evolution of risks communicated?

1226. Recommendation: what do you recommend should be done to ensure that others throughout your organization can benefit from what you have learned?

# Index

260

mandatory    216, 254
manner       136, 149, 184, 215, 236, 238, 245, 248
mantle 120
mapped       32
market 21, 125, 192, 239
marketable   192
marketer     8
marketing    102, 139, 178
markets      23
Maslow       165
material     149-150, 180, 205, 237
materials    1, 143, 208, 222, 226
matrices     141
Matrix  3, 5, 128, 141, 181, 184, 198
matter 33, 44, 50
mattered     256
maximize     193, 229
maximizing   114
McClellan    165
McGregor     165
meaningful   52, 93
measurable   31-32, 124
measure      2, 13, 22, 30, 32, 41-45, 48, 50-51, 53, 57, 65, 68,
70-71, 77-78, 81, 83, 86, 89, 91, 128, 130-131, 174-175, 180, 228
measured     22, 42-44, 47-51, 71, 84-85, 201
measures     42, 45, 47-50, 55, 57, 64, 66, 76, 81, 89, 183, 200,
211, 236
measuring    83, 221
mechanical   1
mechanism    197
mechanisms   130, 182, 249
mediated     226
medium       239
meeting      35, 84, 135, 143, 145, 212, 219, 225-226
meetings     28, 31-32, 35, 136, 188, 218, 226
megatrends   103
member       6, 37, 93, 191, 212, 226, 229
members      28, 32-34, 37, 88, 130, 136, 151, 186, 202, 204,
214, 223-227, 229-230, 235-236
membership   227
mentors      199
message      209
messages     190

sought 128
source 5, 99, 121, 146, 173, 201, 204-205, 221
sources          39, 64, 75, 140
special 89, 125
specific          10, 24, 30-32, 58, 99, 145-146, 155, 158, 161, 177-
178, 204, 207-208, 210, 213, 217, 228, 253
specified          92, 149-151, 237
specify 221, 235
Speech          140
spoken 116
sponsor          23, 134, 151, 206, 246
sponsored          36
sponsors          21, 188, 224, 235, 241
stability 47, 144
stabilize          193
stable   193
staffed 27
staffing 22, 90
stages   188, 220
stakes   129
standard          8, 89, 161, 171, 237, 243-244
standards          1, 12-13, 87, 91, 135, 145-146, 149, 151, 180, 183,
217
started 10, 158-159
starting 13
start-up          224
stated   101, 116, 164, 187, 208
statement          3, 13, 69, 74, 143-144, 146, 220
statements          14, 26, 32, 34, 40, 53, 60, 67, 79, 91, 121, 137-138,
242
states   55
status   6-7, 59, 118, 128, 194, 212, 237, 239-240, 243
stolen   58, 65
storage          182, 215
stored   56, 249
strategic          84, 111, 135, 195, 229, 242
strategies          82, 117, 121, 169, 189, 219, 230
strategy          20, 146, 190, 195, 203, 209, 218, 238, 253
strengths          146, 158, 204
stretch 104
strict    249
strive   104
strong   186

Lightning Source UK Ltd.
Milton Keynes UK
UKHW020615020719
345420UK00010B/435/P